QUIET MOMENTS
of
Encouragement
for
MOMS

QUIET MOMENTS
of
Encouragement
for
MOMS

Ellen Banks Elwell

CROSSWAY BOOKS • WHEATON, ILLINOIS
A DIVISION OF GOOD NEWS PUBLISHERS

Quiet Moments of Encouragement for Moms

Copyright © 1999 by Ellen Banks Elwell

Published by Crossway Books
　　　　　A division of Good News Publishers
　　　　　1300 Crescent Street
　　　　　Wheaton, Illinois 60187

Cover and interior designed by: Design Point Inc.

First printing, 1999

Printed in the United States of America

Library of Congress Cataloging-in-Publication Data

Elwell, Ellen Banks, 1952-
　　　Quiet moments of encouragement for moms / Ellen Banks Elwell.
　　　　　p.　cm.
　　　Includes bibliographical references.
　　　ISBN 1-58134-128-8 (hardcover : alk. paper)
　　　1. Mothers Prayer-books and devotions—English.　2. Devotional calendars.　I. Title.
　　　BV4847.E56　1999
　　　242'.6431—dc21　　　　　　　　　　　　　　　　　99-35238
　　　　　　　　　　　　　　　　　　　　　　　　　　　　　　CIP

15	14	13	12	11	10	09	08	07	06	05	04	03	02	01	00	99
15	14	13	12	11	10	9	8	7	6	5	4	3	2	1		

To

Denise Gill

and

Dori Perrine,

two encouraging women

Contents

Introduction

*A*fter World War II, German students volunteered to help
rebuild a cathedral in England, one of many casualties of
the Luftwaffe bombings. As the work progressed, debate
broke out on how to best restore a large statue of Jesus
with His arms outstretched and bearing the familiar
inscription, "Come unto Me." Careful patching could
repair all damage to the statue except for Christ's hands,
which had been destroyed by bomb fragments. Should
they attempt the delicate task of reshaping those hands?

Finally the workers reached a decision that still stands
today. The statue of Jesus had no hands, and the
inscription now reads, "Christ has no hands but ours."[1]

Christian mothers certainly minister as the hands of
Christ to children, husbands, and friends. Do those around
us see Jesus in *us*? They will if we are becoming more like
Him by getting to know Him through His Word. As we
spend time reading and thinking about the Bible, we
receive encouragement for ourselves and grow in our desire
to be an encouragement to others.

Quiet Moments of Encouragement for Moms includes five
devotional readings per week, all related to a weekly topic,
with suggested Bible readings for weekends or extra days.
Some readings address the mother-child relationship

directly, while others focus on the growth of our souls as women. Each daily reading begins with a Bible verse or verses and ends with a short prayer, encouraging us to extend our thanks, needs, confessions, and praise to God, who loves us immeasurably and wants us to spend time with Him.

My hope is that this book will present truth, offer encouragement, give direction, and promote hope. As a result of spending more time with Christ, may we, members of His body, be the hands of Christ to our children.

Ellen Banks Elwell, 1999

1

Encouragement

ONE

Encouragement

*on't scold your children so much that they
become discouraged and quit trying.*
COLOSSIANS 3:21, TLB

The story is told of a teacher who asked her class what each
wanted to become when they grew up. "President." "A
fireman." "A teacher." One by one they answered until it
was Billy's turn. The teacher asked, "Billy, what do you
want to be when you grow up?" "Possible," Billy
responded. "Possible?" asked the teacher. "Yes," Billy said.
"My mom is always telling me I'm impossible. When I grow
up I want to become *possible*."

Encouragement and discouragement are worlds apart.
In fact, they are downright *opposite*. Encouragement brings
a boost, comfort, cheer, faith, hope, optimism, support, and
trust, whereas discouragement brings a loss of confidence,
dejection, sadness, and pessimism.

It doesn't take me long to decide that I want to be the
encouraging kind of mom, *not* the discouraging kind. But
where do I get help? God's Word is a great place to start.

Anxious hearts are very heavy but a word of encouragement does wonders! (Proverbs 12:25, TLB)

A wise woman builds her house, while a foolish woman tears hers down by her own efforts. (Proverbs 14:1, TLB)

Gentle words cause life and health; griping brings discouragement. (Proverbs 15:4, TLB)

I remember a song by the Gaithers that my children listened to when they were little:

> *I am a promise, I am a possibility,*
> *I am a promise with a capital P.*
> *I am a great big bundle of po-ten-ti-al-i-ty!*

We parents also have potential—the potential to encourage or discourage our children. How are we doing?

Father,
Please forgive us for the times we have discouraged our children. May we choose to apologize, and then look to You and Your Word for the strength to be encouraging! Amen.

TWO

Encouragement

hen I heard what sounded like a great multitude, like the roar of rushing waters and like loud peals of thunder, shouting: "Hallelujah! For our Lord God Almighty reigns."

REVELATION 19:6

My eleven-year-old son was seated next to me in our van when the tape we were listening to began to play the "Hallelujah Chorus" from Handel's *Messiah*. As Jordan took off his seat belt and tried to stand up, we laughed! *Everyone* knows that you stand when you hear the "Hallelujah Chorus," right? But not everyone knows of Handel's discouragement leading up to that composition.

George Frideric Handel's father was a barber who was determined that his son would become a lawyer. In spite of the fact that Handel loved music as a child, his father forbade him to take lessons. That changed when a duke who heard nine-year-old Handel play the organ strongly encouraged the father to give the boy formal music training.

Although he was enormously gifted as an organist and composer, Handel didn't have an easy existence. He fell in and out of favor with changing monarchs, dealt with unpredictable audiences, and was so in debt that he thought he might end up in prison. Terribly discouraged, Handel was ready to retire from public life when he received a libretto taken entirely from the Bible that came at the same time that he received a commission from a Dublin charity to compose for a benefit performance.

Handel began composing, and after twenty-four days he completed 260 pages of a manuscript, titled *Messiah*. One writer commented that the music and message of *Messiah* "has probably done more to convince thousands of mankind that there is a God . . . than all the theological works ever written."[2]

Just because we're discouraged doesn't mean God can't use us!

God who sees the whole picture,
It's easy for us to give up and lose heart when we're discouraged. Help us to run to You and to remember that many people who have contributed to expanding Your kingdom were at some points discouraged people. Amen.

THREE

Encouragement

*But encourage one another daily, as long as it is called Today, so that
none of you may be hardened by sin's deceitfulness.*

HEBREWS 3:13

To understand the encouragement we are taught to give to
one another, we must look at what the author of Hebrews
wrote just prior to this verse. "See to it, brothers, that none
of you has a sinful, unbelieving heart that turns away from
the living God." The children of Israel had contempt for
God, and this displayed itself through negativism,
grumbling, quarreling, and disobedience.

> Many of those, perhaps most, who left in the Exodus had
> an inadequate faith in God. At first, due to their miserable
> plight of 430 years of slavery, the brilliant leadership of
> Moses, the repeated miraculous plagues on Pharaoh, and
> the grand miracles of the pillars of cloud and fire and the
> parting of the sea, they were ready to follow God
> anywhere. But as soon as the initial glow wore off, they
> outrageously cried, "Is the Lord among us or not?"
> (Exodus 17:7). It was a fair-weather, herd-instinct faith —
> good until the first trial, when it dissolved in unbelief.[3]

So how do we encourage each other? First, we support each other. We come alongside a fellow struggler with understanding and help. Another way of stimulating and inspiring one another to have hope and courage is by sharing God's Word and praying. When my children are going through difficulties, I sometimes jot down for them specific Bible verses I am praying in regard to their circumstances. This can also be helpful for husbands, for friends, and even for ourselves. Whom can we encourage today?

Father,
Thanks for the encouragement we have received from fellow believers in times of personal discouragement. Thank You that through the influence of Your Word, others helped us with reality checks. Please help us to be an encouragement to those around us. Amen.

FOUR

Encouragement

Why are you downcast, O my soul? Why so disturbed within me? Put your hope in God, for I will yet praise him, my Savior and my God.
PSALM 42:11

Only those intimately acquainted with sheep and their habits understand the significance of a "cast" sheep or a "cast down" sheep. This is an old English shepherd's term for a sheep that has turned over on its back and cannot get up again by itself. A "cast" sheep is a very pathetic sight. Lying on its back, its feet in the air, it flays away frantically struggling to stand up, without success. Sometimes it will bleat a little for help, but generally it lies there lashing about in frightened frustration.[4]

A sheep becomes downcast when it lies down and its center of gravity shifts so that its feet no longer touch the ground. At this point the sheep frequently panics, realizing that it is impossible to regain its footing on its own. In the heat of the summer, a cast-down sheep can die in a few hours. In cooler weather it might survive a few days. Shepherds are constantly on the lookout for this problem, and that is one of the reasons they count their sheep and search for any that are missing.

We too sometimes become downcast, realizing that our center of gravity has shifted and we cannot get our feet back on the ground. Only our Shepherd can stand us upright and get our blood circulating again. He doesn't rush toward us with a rod to beat us, but He tenderly sets us upright and longs that we would choose to follow Him. What a kind Shepherd we have!

Father,
Thank You that You are our Good Shepherd and that You deal with us tenderly. Amen.

FIVE

Encouragement

Be merciful, O Lord, for I am looking up to you in constant hope.

PSALM 86:3, TLB

When our young children are hurt, sad, lonely, or confused, they often run to us. But when we moms are hurt, sad, lonely, or confused, where do *we* run?

I love the words to a song I learned in college:

> *Where shall I run, Lord, when all around me, trouble and strife seem to be everywhere? Haven't you said that you would protect me? Safe in your hand I will evermore be. With such protection, none can alarm me, though the storms of life almost kill. Ever to this shelter I will be fleeing. No other one can provide peace for me.*[5]

The next time we feel hurt, sad, lonely, or confused, we can write out the following verses and read them throughout the day to encourage our souls:

> *All those who know your mercy, Lord, will count on you for help. For you have never yet forsaken those who trust in you. (Psalm 9:10, TLB)*

> *Blessed is the Lord, for he has shown me that his never-failing love protects me like the walls of a fort! (Psalm 31:21, TLB)*

My protection and success come from God alone. He is my refuge, a Rock where no enemy can reach me. O my people, trust him all the time. Pour out your longings before him, for he can help! (Psalm 62:7-8, TLB)

Lord, when doubts fill my mind, when my heart is in turmoil, quiet me and give me renewed hope and cheer. (Psalm 94:19, TLB)

Father,
Thank You that no matter where we are—sitting in the car, standing at the sink, lying in bed, or walking outside, we can run to You anytime we need encouragement. Thank You that You renew us with Your presence and Your Word. Amen.

EXTRA READINGS FOR DAYS 6 AND 7
Psalm 42; Psalm 86

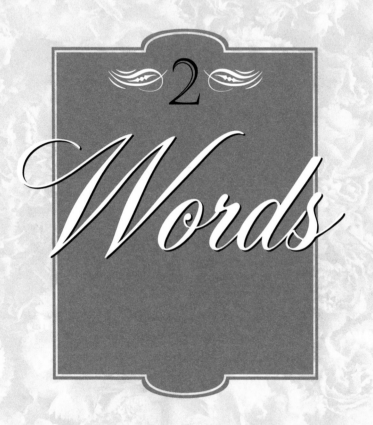

2

Words

ONE

Words

He who guards his mouth and his tongue keeps himself from calamity.
PROVERBS 21:23

The story is told of a young man during the Middle Ages who went to a monk, saying, "I've sinned by telling slanderous statements about someone. What should I do now?" The monk replied, "Put a feather on every doorstep in town." The young man did just that. He then came back to the monk wondering if there was anything else he should do. The monk said, "Go back and pick up all those feathers." The young man replied excitedly, "That's impossible! By now the wind will have blown them all over town!" The monk said, "So has your slanderous word become impossible to retrieve."[6]

To slander is to speak falsely of someone and hurt his reputation. This can happen in many different ways, possibly most often when we jump to conclusions or join our children in jumping to conclusions about another person. If the conclusion we come to regarding someone else is false, we have been guilty of slander.

Sometimes we forget that slander is prohibited in the

Ninth Commandment: "You shall not give false testimony against your neighbor" (Exodus 20:16) The commandments about lying, stealing, or adultery seem to stand out more, but God hates slander because the devil does it too — about us! Satan is called the great accuser because he opposes Christians and accuses us before God.

Since we don't like the idea of being falsely accused, we're wise to be equally as careful about protecting the reputation of others. Once the feathers are distributed, they can't be easily retrieved.

Father,
Please help us to guard our mouths from slandering others. Amen.

TWO
Words

With the tongue we praise our Lord and Father, and with it we curse men, who have been made in God's likeness. Out of the same mouth come praise and cursing. My brothers, this should not be. Can both fresh water and salt water flow from the same spring? My brothers, can a fig tree bear olives, or a grapevine bear figs? Neither can a salt spring produce fresh water.
JAMES 3:9-12

If you have a telephone in your home, you probably have many telemarketers calling (bombarding?) you each week. Sometimes I receive as many as four or five sales calls in one day! Some of the callers can be quite persistent, so my response calls for determination mixed with graciousness.

I have noticed that the callers are frequently caught by surprise if I answer on the first ring. This past week I picked up one call after the first ring and answered, "Hello!" I heard silence, and then a man used the name of God in a disgusted way. I repeated, "Hello?" a second time, and then, a bit startled, the man turned on his professional phone voice and said, "Well, hello, Mrs. Elwell" and launched into his pitch.

No matter how fine a salesman he was, he lost me back at the beginning of the call because of the way he spoke God's name. At a point when he stopped to take a breath, I kindly explained that I wasn't interested in his product, and in addition I had been offended by the way he had spoken God's name into the telephone at the outset of the call. In a sugary voice he said, "God *bless* you, ma'am!" and hung up. The tone at the end of the call sure didn't match the words at the beginning.

Our children are listening to us each day to see how consistent *we* are. Since the words that come out of our mouths reveal what's in our hearts, what are our words saying about our hearts?

Father,
"Set a guard over my mouth, O LORD; keep watch over the door of my lips. Let not my heart be drawn to what is evil" (Psalm 141:3-4).

THREE

Words

*Reckless words pierce like a sword, but the tongue of
the wise brings healing.*

PROVERBS 12:18

Walter Wangerin, in his collection of short stories *Ragman
and Other Cries of Faith*, begins one of his stories with what
seems to be a lesson in entomology, the study of insects
(specifically spiders). But he surprisingly turns it into an
unforgettable metaphor of spiritual truth. He explains
that a female spider is often a widow for embarrassing
reasons—she regularly eats those who come her way.
Lonely suitors and visitors alike quickly become corpses
so that her dining room is a morgue. A visiting fly, having
become captive, will be granted the illusion of wholeness,
but she will have drunk his insides so that he has become
his own hollow casket.

This is a gruesome but effective metaphor to describe
the destructive power of evilly intended words. Words
that do not dissolve mere organs and nerves but souls!
This world is populated by walking caskets because
countless lives have been dissolved and sucked empty by
another's words.[7]

We know that words can kill because most of us have been on the giving end and the receiving end. As a mom I want to be careful how I speak to my own children and what I say about them to others, because words can build my children up or tear them down. In our families it's one thing to hear a life situation discussed with discernment, but it's another thing to hear it recounted with criticism. When we judge another, God tells us we're setting ourselves above Him—an arrogant, scary place to be. We want our words to encourage people's souls, not dissolve them.

Father,
Please forgive me for the times my words have hurt others. May I not set myself above Your law by criticizing and judging others. Amen.

FOUR

Words

A fool's talk brings a rod to his back, but the lips of the wise protect them.

PROVERBS 14:3

I remember one exciting Christmas as a child when one of my younger sisters received a Chatty Cathy doll. If we pulled the cord on the doll's back, she spoke preset sentences. What fun we had! In real life God has not programmed us with only a few phrases that we repeat throughout our lives (although our kids might accuse us of repetition sometimes!). He gave us the words of the language we have learned. How precious to choose words for their creativity, not for protection or harm. To inspire us in our word choices, let's look at what God's Word has to say about our words:

Evil words destroy. Godly skill rebuilds. (Proverb 11:9, TLB)

The upright speak what is helpful; the wicked speak rebellion. (Proverb 10:32, TLB)

Kind words are like honey—enjoyable and healthful. (Proverb 16:24, TLB)

Fire goes out for lack of fuel, and tensions disappear when gossip stops. (Proverbs 26:20, TLB)

In the end, people appreciate frankness more than flattery. (Proverbs 28:23, TLB)

When she speaks, her words are wise, and kindness is the rule for everything she says. (Proverbs 31:26, TLB)

A wise man holds his tongue. Only a fool blurts out everything he knows; that only leads to sorrow and trouble. (Proverbs 10:14, TLB)

A gossip goes around spreading rumors, while a trustworthy man tries to quiet them. (Proverbs 11:13, TLB)

Your own soul is nourished when you are kind; it is destroyed when you are cruel. (Proverbs 11:17, TLB)

With the inspiration of God's Word and the strength of God's help, may we make word choices today that protect, not harm!

Father,
May we choose words from our language that protect and encourage.
Amen.

FIVE

Words

A gentle answer turns away wrath, but a harsh word stirs up anger.
PROVERBS 15:1

Before our third son was born, my husband and I and two sons took a week's vacation to Petoskey, Michigan. The second day of our vacation, I had a severe allergic reaction and ended up in the local hospital for three days while my husband tried to occupy Chad and Nate, then seven and five. Let's say it was not one of our more memorable vacations! I felt alone, scared, and disappointed that our plans were ruined, and Jim had to play "Mr. Mom" for those days. But any hard experience also has lessons for good that we can take away with us, and this event was no exception.

The elderly woman that I shared the hospital room with was quite confused, to put it mildly. Although the curtain between our beds was drawn shut, for three days I heard a lot of different voices from a variety of nurses and doctors throughout the day and night. One thing I'll never forget was the effect that the words of the medical professionals had on the elderly woman, confused though she was. The gentle and soft words, though spoken with firm and direct voices, were able to get a whole lot more cooperation from the woman than harsh, unpleasant ones.

That principle also holds true for us as moms. In dealing with our children, choosing words and tones that are considerate and compassionate will reap better results than words that are rough or strident.

Father,
May my words be gentle and not harsh. Amen.

EXTRA READINGS FOR DAYS 6 AND 7
James 3:1-12; Ecclesiastes 5:2-7

3

Courage

ONE

Courage

*Then his sister asked Pharaoh's daughter, "Shall I go and get one of the
Hebrew women to nurse the baby for you?"*
EXODUS 2:7

Courage is found not only in older people, but in young
people too. Consider Miriam, the sister of Moses. Moses'
mother, Jochebed, decided to do a very bold thing. In order
to protect Moses from being killed by Pharaoh's soldiers,
she wove some reeds into a small basket. Perhaps Miriam
wondered what her mother was making—until she found
out that the basket would cradle her baby brother as he
floated down the river. Miriam probably saw her mother
weeping as she kissed her infant son and laid him in the
basket, putting it into the water. I can only wonder what
thoughts and feelings were going on inside Miriam as she
stood on the riverbank, watching from a distance.

You know the rest of the story. Pharaoh's daughter
found the baby when she went to the river to bathe, and
Miriam ran to her, asking if she should find a Hebrew
mother (her own!) to nurse the baby. What a courageous
thing for a child to do! The courage she exercised as a

young girl no doubt prompted her own growth in faith. Imagine all the times that she and Jochebed must have rehearsed that story together through the years. Later in the book of Exodus we read that Miriam led the children of Israel in song after the crossing of the Red Sea.

It's very difficult for mothers to sit back and watch their children struggle through difficult situations. We'd much rather protect them from pain or risk. But as we see in Miriam, courage can spring from childhood difficulties, resulting in personal faith and leadership down the road.

Father,
When we know or sense that our child is struggling with some difficulty, please give us great wisdom as moms to know how much to guide them, how much or how little to say, and how much to stand back, waiting to see You work in their hearts and lives! Amen.

TWO

Courage

he LORD turned to him and said, "Go in the strength you have and save Israel out of Midian's hand. Am I not sending you?"

JUDGES 6:14

After forty years of freedom, the children of Israel again began worshiping idols. As a result the Midianites took over the land of Israel, treating the people poorly. When the Israelites cried out to God, God chose Gideon to help them.

One day when Gideon was threshing wheat, an angel from God visited him and stated, "The LORD is with you, mighty warrior." Gideon responded, "But sir, if the LORD is with us, why has all this happened to us? Where are all the wonders that our fathers told us about when they said, 'Did not the LORD bring us up out of Egypt?' But now the LORD has abandoned us and put us into the hand of Midian."

The perspective here is curious. God called Gideon a *"mighty warrior,"* but Gideon initially saw himself as *abandoned.* Gideon perceived his clan to be the weakest in Manasseh, and he thought himself to be the least in his family. But God promised Gideon His presence and His strength and agreed to Gideon's request for a sign of confirmation. After God's confirmation, Gideon was willing to serve God, and God used him in incredible and powerful ways to get the Israelites back on track and defeat the Midianites.

Have you ever thought of yourself as weak or abandoned? Being human, we all experience these feelings from time to time. But when we get a glimpse of God, we realize that His presence and His strength are more than enough to accomplish what needs to be done in our part of God's bigger plan for the world!

Father,
Thanks that You were patient with Gideon's questions and that You're patient with us too. When we feel weak or abandoned, may we run to You, get a glimpse of Your power, and realize Your presence and strength in our lives. Amen.

THREE

Courage

Our lives for your lives!" the men assured her. "If you don't tell what we are doing, we will treat you kindly and faithfully when the LORD gives us the land."

JOSHUA 2:14

I remember seeing flannelgraph pictures of Rahab the harlot when I heard the Bible story told as a young child. Joshua sent two spies to Jericho, and Rahab secretly housed them and helped them escape by hiding them on her roof under stalks of flax. Later Rahab lowered the two spies down the outside wall through the window of her house. She was a woman of courage as she took great risk in hiding the spies. As a result of her help, she and her family were later spared death.

It's interesting that Rahab called God "the Lord" in her conversation with the spies.

> *"I know that the LORD has given this land to you and that a great fear of you has fallen on us, so that all who live in this country are melting in fear because of you." (Joshua 2:9)*

Rahab was not saved from physical or spiritual destruction because of her character or her works. Rather she was saved through her faith. Any woman who has had major struggles with character or behavior can find great hope and encouragement from the life of Rahab. She was a sinner who was saved through her faith, and she proved her faith by courageously risking her life to protect God's people, eventually bringing her family to faith in God. She was noted for her faith in the Hebrews 11 "Hall of Faith," and amazingly, because of her marriage into a Jewish family, she became part of the ancestry of Jesus (Matthew 1:5).

Father,
To trace Rahab back in Your ancestry is encouraging to us, demonstrating that people with a sinful past can be transformed. Thank You for her example of courage, which was born through faith in You. Amen.

Courage

Look," said Naomi, "your sister-in-law is going back to her people and her gods. Go back with her." But Ruth replied, "Don't urge me to leave you or to turn back from you. Where you go I will go, and where you stay I will stay. Your people will be my people and your God my God."

RUTH 1:15-16

Woven throughout the Bible are stories of courage—stories of small people who accomplished great things in God's strength. God's plans and purposes are carried from one generation to another with amazing twists, turns, and surprises, and Ruth was part of one of those plans!

A woman who had grown up in Moab, Ruth married a Jewish man, Mahlon, one of the sons of Elimelech. Elimelech, his wife Naomi, and their two sons had left Israel to escape a famine, and while they were in Moab, both sons married Moabite girls. Sadly, Elimelech and both sons died, leaving Naomi and two daughters-in-law as widows. Naomi decided to return to her hometown of Bethlehem, assuming Ruth and Orpah would prefer to stay in Moab. But because of Ruth's love for Naomi, she insisted on going along.

An industrious woman, Ruth gleaned grain that had been dropped by harvesters in the field of Boaz, bringing it back to Naomi to bake bread. When Boaz found out who Ruth was, he offered her much more than the leftovers. He was kind to her because of her kindness to Naomi.

In God's plan, Ruth and Boaz ended up marrying, and a few generations later Ruth became the great-grandmother of King David. Because she had the courage to leave her homeland, accompany her mother-in-law back to Israel, and work to provide for her mother-in-law, God blessed her life. What a beautiful story of love and courage!

Father,
Thank You for the intricate ways Your plans unfold from one generation to another. Thank You that we can read these stories in Your Word and be reminded of Your great love and faithfulness. May we have faith to believe that You are weaving Your purposes into our lives, and courage to obey. Amen.

FIVE

Courage

"And if I perish, I perish."
ESTHER 4:16

Esther was the woman of the hour. A Jewish woman, she had been chosen by the king to be his new queen—but he didn't know she was Jewish. Esther's cousin, Mordecai, overheard a plot by wicked Haman. Haman went to the impulsive king and proposed that he would pay the equivalent of 100,000 dollars into the king's treasury in exchange for the destruction of the Jews. In God's gracious providence, Mordecai was able to communicate this plan to Esther. Because Mordecai believed God's promises and dared to act, Esther ultimately decided to go to the king on behalf of the Jews. This was a great risk because protocol dictated that anyone going to the king without having been invited could be killed instantly, unless the king held out his golden scepter. Before going, Esther asked her people to gather together for three days of fasting. Then she said, "If I die, I die."

In the meantime Haman had constructed a gallows on which he planned to hang Mordecai. But because of

Esther's courage and trust in God's plan to save the Jews, Haman's evil was eventually exposed, and in a great reversal the king used the gallows to hang Haman.

It's important for us to see that Esther's courage was not in herself. Rather, she was waiting on God's providence and strength. We don't beat Satan and his schemes with courage we come up with ourselves. We thank God that because of Christ's victory over death and sin on the cross, the devil's schemes can be defeated in our lives.

God our Preserver,
Thank You that the One who is in us is greater than the One who is in the world. Please give us Your courage as we face struggles within our own families. Thanks for the victory only You can give in defeating the devil's schemes. Amen.

EXTRA READINGS FOR DAYS 6 AND 7
Judges 6; Exodus 2:1-10

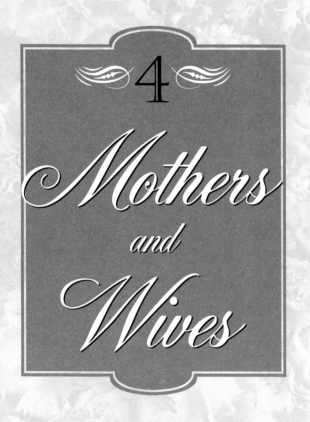

4

Mothers

and

Wives

ONE

Mothers and Wives

*The virgin will be with child and will give birth to a son, and they will
call him Immanuel" — which means, "God with us."*

MATTHEW 1:23

As I write this devotional it's January, and the Christmas
season is still lingering in my mind. Because I am a mom,
one of the Christmas themes I enjoy thinking about is
motherhood. Jesus had a mother! When we look at the
New Testament accounts of the life of Christ, we don't
have to search far to see the important role his mother had
in his life.

From the Annunciation to Pentecost, Mary was focused
on her child. She nursed him in Bethlehem, fled with him
to Egypt, took him to the temple for his religious training
and watched as he grew independent of her. The fact that
they were still close as late as the miracle at Cana suggests
that she was by then a widow, relying on him as her oldest
son. She accepted his rebuff, followed him on his travels,
seeking to protect him even then. When he announced
that the mother or brother was not flesh and blood but a
part of the family of faith, she appears to have accepted
this new relationship, continuing as his disciple until she

stood at the foot of the cross. Testimony to her transformed relationship, from flesh and blood to spiritual follower, is in her presence in the upper room, where she waited for the Holy Spirit with his other disciples.[8]

When we struggle as moms, when we're unsure of our roles, when we need wisdom and help for a particular stage, it is so comforting to remember that the One to whom we pray is also One who *had a mother!*

Jesus,
Thank You that You understand our challenges from both a human and a divine perspective. May we look to You for help and wisdom in dealing with things that You observed and experienced Yourself. Thank You that You are "God with us." Amen.

TWO
Mothers and Wives

She watches over the affairs of her household and does not eat the bread of idleness.
PROVERBS 31:27

Too many times women are made to feel that they should apologize for being mothers and housewives. In reality, such roles can be noble callings. When I was on the faculty of the University of Pennsylvania, there were gatherings from time to time to which faculty members brought their spouses. Inevitably, some woman lawyer or sociologist would confront my wife with the question, "And what is it that you do, my dear?" My wife, who is one of the most brilliantly articulate individuals I know, had a great response: "I am socializing two homo-sapiens in the dominant values of the Judeo-Christian tradition in order that they might be instruments for the trans-formation of the social order into the teleologically prescribed utopia inherent in the eschaton." When she followed that with, "And what is it that you do?" the other person's "a lawyer" just wasn't that overpowering.[9]

I love that story! We can become so weary of doing the menial tasks that it's easy to lose sight of the great privilege

God has given us—to influence and mold young lives for His kingdom. Tucked away near the end of my church's hymnal are some words that I love to sing, but I never sing them without tears in my eyes and a lump in my throat.

> *Lord of life and King of glory,*
> *Who didst deign a child to be,*
> *Cradled on a mother's bosom,*
> *Throned upon a mother's knee:*
> *For the children Thou hast given*
> *We must answer unto Thee.*[10]

Lord of life,
Thank You for the gift of children. We are so rich. Please empower us with Your love, strength, and wisdom so we will raise children who will help to further Your kingdom. Amen.

THREE

Mothers and Wives

We will tell the next generation the praiseworthy deeds of the LORD, his power, and the wonders he has done.

PSALM 78:4

Max Jukes lived in New York. He did not believe in Christ or in Christian training. He refused to take his children to church, even when they asked to go. He has had 1,026 descendants; 300 were sent to prison for an average term of thirteen years; 190 were public prostitutes; 680 were admitted alcoholics. His family, thus far, has cost the state in excess of $420,000. They made no contributions to society.

Jonathan Edwards lived in the same state, at the same time as Jukes. He loved the Lord and saw that his children were in church every Sunday, as he served the Lord to the best of his ability. He has had 929 descendants, and of these 430 were ministers; 86 became university professors; 13 became university presidents; 75 authored good books; 7 were elected to the United States Congress. One was Vice President of his nation. His family never cost the state one cent but has contributed immeasurably to the life of plenty in this land today.[11]

What kind of heritage are we leaving for *our* children? Down the road, we'd all like to leave our children some kind of monetary inheritance or a few pieces of furniture that will hold sentimental value. But we'd be wise to focus more on the inheritance with a value that cannot be measured.

Will we pass down a love for God and His Word—an example of truth, love, and mercy—a grateful heart? These are the most valuable gifts we can give.

Father,
In our busy days as moms, please help us to think ahead to the kind of
inheritance we wish to leave for our children. Amen.

Mothers and Wives

*A quarrelsome wife is like a constant dripping on a rainy day;
restraining her is like restraining the wind or
grasping oil with the hand.*

PROVERBS 27:15-16

We've all seen sitcoms or comic strips about dominating mothers or wives, and we've probably known a few in real life as well. Not surprisingly, the Bible includes some accounts of dominating and difficult-to-live-with women that we can learn from. Let's look at a few.

Rebekah tries to outwit her decrepit husband and pushes her compliant son Jacob into a plot to deceive his father in the celebrated case of the stolen blessing (Gen. 27). Later, Potiphar's wife, skillful in perpetrating treachery against the virtuous servant Joseph, uses racial rhetoric to inflame her husband to imprison Joseph, contrary to anything he would have done if left to his own designs (Gen. 39:6-20).

Later, the Old Testament history provides further examples. Delilah, though never technically identified as a wife, plays the role of the domineering female by contriving to rob Samson of his strength and deliver him into the power of her compatriots (Judg. 16). Solomon provides the most extravagant example of all: his one thousand wives and concubines "turned away his heart after other gods." (I Kings 11:4). The wicked Jezebel dominates her husband Ahab by inclining him toward pagan religious practices (I Kings 16:29-33) and by grabbing the initiative in seizing Naboth's vineyard for her pouting husband (I Kings 21).[12]

To see women who have used their influence over men for deception, evil, or destruction is not a pretty picture, and yet it is not difficult for us to repeat those behaviors in our own families. Only the wisdom and strength of God will help us avoid falling into these negative patterns ourselves. May we humbly ask for His help *each day!*

Father,
"May the words of my mouth and the meditation of my heart be pleasing in your sight, O LORD, my Rock and my Redeemer" (Psalm 19:14). Amen.

FIVE

Mothers and Wives

ives, in the same way be submissive to your husbands so that,
if any of them do not believe the word, they may be won over
without talk by the behavior of their wives, when they see
the purity and reverence of your lives.

1 PETER 3:1-2

Some would see these verses to hand a wife the role of a doormat, but as we take a closer look, that's not what we find. A wife is not a powerless woman; rather, she is much more powerful than she sometimes realizes. In these verses Peter was speaking to the woman in the Roman world.

Under Roman law, the husband and father had absolute authority over all members of his household, including his wife. If he disapproved of her new beliefs, she could endanger her marriage by demanding her rights as a free woman in Christ. Peter reassured Christian women married to unbelievers that they did not need to preach to their husbands. Under the circumstances, their best approach would be loving service: they should show their husbands the kind of self-giving love that Christ showed the church.[13]

The woman who thinks she can persuade her husband with *words* is mistaken. Rather, he is influenced by the way she conducts herself—her ethics, her habits, her morals, and her dealings. "Purity" means being free from pollution, abuse, or contamination. "Reverence" includes awe for God, respect for others, and the realization that God created her with great value.

Wives are instructed to go along with their husbands, but not to allow abuse. Allowing abuse of any kind to go on would contradict God's instruction to be pure, meaning "free of abuse or pollution." Whether a husband is an unbeliever or a believer who is acting like an unbeliever, actions speak louder than words.

Father,
May we never forget the tremendous influence and persuasion that we have as wives. Please help us grow in purity and reverence, remembering that our behavior can be winsome. Amen.

EXTRA READINGS FOR DAYS 6 AND 7
Psalm 78:1-8; 1 Peter 3:1-9

5

Friendship

ONE

Friendship

At that time Mary got ready and hurried to a town in the hill country of Judah, where she entered Zechariah's home and greeted Elizabeth.

LUKE 1:39-40

Think about your close friendships. What are some of the ingredients that make them special? My list would include common values, enjoyable companionship, mutual respect, shared circumstances, and exchanged confidences.

In Luke 1 we see that during the months before and after the births of John the Baptist and Jesus, Elizabeth and Mary formed a special friendship. The Bible explains that Elizabeth was a woman who was obedient to God's Word, and in the reaction of Mary to the angel's announcement, we see evidence of her humility, belief in God, and willingness to be His servant.

The circumstances these women shared were remarkably similar. Both women's pregnancies were announced by angels, and both were unusual—Elizabeth's because she was old, and Mary's because she was a virgin. Both women were obedient to God's Word and were willing to be His servants.

I love Luke 1:39's describing how Mary "hurried" to the town where Elizabeth lived. That's how it is when we enjoy the companionship of another woman—we can't *wait* to share our news!

Mary and Elizabeth must have had many cups of tea and hours of deep conversation as they shared the secrets of their own experiences—the angels, the announcements, the wonder, and the pregnancies. The mutual respect between these two women was fascinating. If they had been petty or selfish women, there might have been some jealousy. But instead we find Elizabeth, who was full of God's Spirit, blessing Mary, and Mary, who was full of belief, praising God. They were truly soul mates whose souls were aligned first with God and then with each other. What a wonderful example of Christian friendship these women have left for us today!

Father,
Thank You for the companionship, respect, shared circumstances, and confidences modeled in the friendship of Mary and Elizabeth. Please provide us with the blessing of Christian friends, and give us grace to be the best friend we can be. Amen.

TWO

Friendship

Your own soul is nourished when you are kind; it is destroyed when you are cruel.

PROVERBS 11:17, TLB

A young soldier in World War I asked his officer to allow him to go out into the "no man's land" between the trenches to bring in one of his comrades who lay grievously wounded. "You can go," said the officer, "but it's not worth it. Your friend is probably dead, and you will throw your own life away." But the man went. Somehow he managed to get to his friend, hoist him onto his shoulder, and bring him back to the trenches. The two of them tumbled in together and lay at the bottom. The officer looked very tenderly on the would-be rescuer, and then he said, "I told you it wouldn't be worth it. Your friend is dead, and you are mortally wounded." "It was worth it though, sir," he said. "How do you mean, 'worth it'? I tell you, your friend is dead." "Yes, sir," the boy answered, "but it was worth it because when I got to him he was still alive, and he said to me, 'Jim, I knew you'd come.'"

Isn't that the kind of friend each of us desires? That

kind of friend sees a need, is willing to get involved, and acts unselfishly.

In God's gracious plan, we are sometimes the givers and sometimes the receivers. Healthy friendships involve a certain degree of both and are worth more than their weight in gold! May we be challenged to be that kind of friend.

Father,
Thank You for the wonderful gift of friendship. For that mom who is lonely or new to a community, please provide a friend to bring grace into her life. And may we be sensitive to the hurts and needs of our friends around us. Amen.

THREE

Friendship

*"Greater love has no one than this, that one
lay down his life for his friends."*
JOHN 15:13

What kind of a friend was Jesus? Several years ago I looked through the Gospels to find answers to that question. Here are some of the discoveries I made:

1. Jesus took *initiative*—He called out to Peter and Andrew.

2. He spent time (lots of it) with those He taught. And He talked about the really important things in life.

3. He reached out and *touched* the man with leprosy—He was compassionate.

4. Jesus was a man who associated with sinners. When the Pharisees asked Him about this, He explained that it's not the healthy who need a doctor—it's the sick people.

5. He was *honest* with his friends and separated himself from false flattery.

6. He was protective but not in a temporal sense—He was protective of people's souls.

7. He served His friends, leaving them an example by washing their feet.

8. He prayed for His friends, that they would be united as God and Jesus are, that they would be kept from Satan's power, and that they would be made pure and holy through the Word. This is a great model of how to pray for our children and their friends.

9. He ultimately sacrificed His lifeblood for sinners—for us.

10. The friends that Jesus did not choose were people who pretended to be good when they weren't, and people who were so obsessed with detailed regulations that they lost sight of justice and the love of God.

What a great example of friendship Jesus left for all of us!

Father,
Thank You that You are the best friend we could ever have. Thanks that You call us Your friends if we obey You. Please help us to be a good friend. Amen.

FOUR

Friendship

*Elisha said, "Go around and ask all your neighbors for empty jars.
Don't ask for just a few."*
2 KINGS 4:3

There is a tendency in each one of us to deny loneliness. We want to live life independently, no leaning on other people. But a nagging sense of loneliness keeps getting in the way. Sometimes it becomes so severe we can hardly think about anything else. I believe God created us incomplete, not as a cruel trick to edge us toward self-pity, but as an opportunity to edge us toward others with similar needs. His whole plan for us involves relationships with others: reach out to the world around us in love. Loneliness, that painful twinge inside, makes us reach out.[14]

With all the hustle and bustle of our schedules as moms, we have a fair amount of physical companionship—especially when the children are young. But moms can feel lonely, even when there are lots of bodies in the room, if their souls haven't had enough opportunity to knit with a friend or companion. God built this need into us.

Think of the person in Luke 15 who lost something and

upon finding it rejoiced with friends. Or remember the widow ministered to by Elijah, who was instructed to ask all her friends and neighbors for jars to hold the oil that was about to be miraculously multiplied. Asking her friends for their help may have been difficult or humbling, but what joy and excitement they all shared in the experience!

When we get to feeling lonely, two things are helpful: (1) presenting our need to God because He cares, sees, and provides; and (2) calling a friend or someone we'd like to get to know and puting something on the calendar!

Father,
Thank You that You intend for us to need other people. Thank You that You understand our feelings of loneliness because You experienced it Yourself when You lived on earth. May we do our part in connecting with others around us. Amen.

FIVE

Friendship

A friend loves at all times, and a brother is born for adversity.
PROVERBS 17:17

When I consider my close friendships, three things come to mind: (1) mutual love. None of us is perfect, so we're not looking for perfection, but we must have admiration for our friend's qualities. (2) Mutual trust. If a friendship isn't built on mutual respect and trust, it isn't healthy. God warns us in Proverbs 22:24, "Do not make friends with a hot-tempered man, do not associate with one easily angered, or you may learn his ways and get yourself ensnared." (3) Shared conversations and experiences. Whether funny and lighthearted or deep and serious, we accumulate memories of sharing and caring. Of course, having each experienced the common denominator of God's love and grace adds an eternal element to our friendships.

A friend is someone to whom I do not have to explain myself. Such a friendship offers unspeakable comfort. Friendship can also be redemptive, for friends can act as mediators of God's presence and invite us into the embrace of God's grace.

In some friendships, we must do more giving. It is then that we are called to become midwives for whatever God is bringing to birth in our friends. In other friendships, we are more on the receiving end. It is important to balance our friendships so that sometimes we are the givers and other times we are the receivers.[15]

How do we help our children develop healthy friendships? By our example in the friends we choose, by praying for their friendships, and by guiding and encouraging them to make healthy choices for themselves.

Father,
Thanks that friendships can be redemptive. Please help us to be that kind of friend to those around us. Amen.

EXTRA READINGS FOR DAYS 6 AND 7
Luke 1:1-56; 2 Kings 4:1-7

6

Example

ONE

Example

A patient man has great understanding, but a
quick-tempered man displays folly.
PROVERBS 14:29

What kind of examples are we to our children in the area of patience? I doubt there's a mom alive who doesn't struggle with impatience daily.

I heard a story once about a man whose car stalled in heavy traffic as the light turned green. All his efforts to start the engine failed, and a chorus of honking behind him made matters worse. He finally got out of his car and walked back to the first driver and said, "I'm sorry, but I can't seem to get my car started. If you'll go up there and give it a try, I'll stay here and blow your horn for you!"

The man whose car was stuck was both patient and understanding, whereas the honking man displayed a quick temper and folly. Patient people are usually people of understanding. Because they are not looking out only for themselves, they are generally not hasty or impulsive. When pain, difficulty, or annoyance come into their lives, they are willing to stand back and attempt to perceive the significance of a situation with some degree of calm.

Quick-tempered people, on the other hand, become angry or irritable very quickly and very easily. They lack a good sense of understanding, which stems from their lack of thought about other people's needs.

The more we grow in Christ, the more patient we become, because patience is one of the evidences that God's Spirit is present and working in our lives!

Father,
Thanks for pictures from Your Word showing what patience looks like and what it doesn't look like. Please help us to learn and be good examples to our children. Amen.

TWO

Example

Near the cross of Jesus stood his mother, his mother's sister, Mary the wife of Clopas, and Mary of Magdala. When Jesus saw his mother there, and the disciple whom he loved standing nearby, he said to his mother, "Dear woman, here is your son," and to the disciple, "Here is your mother." From that time on, this disciple took her into his home.

JOHN 19:25-27

In contrast to the soldiers who *had* to be present at the cross of Jesus, John and Jesus' mother, Mary, were there because of love. Jesus and John had been close friends, and Mary and Jesus shared a love that few others understood. In addition to the normal amount of memories that mothers and sons share, Mary and Jesus both knew they were part of God's plan for the world—His plan to provide relationship between God and us.

Leaving us an example for our own relationships, Jesus *noticed*, Jesus *spoke*, and Jesus *provided*. Jesus *noticed* His mother, and Jesus *noticed* His friend. In spite of the fact that He was very near to death and had been hanging on the cross for hours, He noticed. What amazing, selfless love! I sometimes fail to notice other's needs just because I am tired.

Even though it took great effort, Jesus *spoke*. He said to Mary, "Dear woman, here is your son," and to the disciple, "Here is your mother." How touched Mary must have felt that Jesus was using some of His last words to remind her of how much He cared for her.

Jesus *provided* for Mary by asking John to take her home with him. Mary was a widow at that time, and Jesus exercised love and responsibility in wanting to make sure His mother was taken care of.

Jesus' example of *noticing*, *speaking*, and *providing* is one we can follow in all of our friendships and family relationships.

Lord Jesus,
Thank You that even when You were close to death, You noticed, You spoke, and You provided. May we follow Your example. Amen.

THREE

Example

A beautiful woman lacking discretion and modesty is like a fine gold ring in a pig's snout.

PROVERBS 11:22, TLB

Earth mothers and sex kittens. Frumpy housewives and pants-suited career girls. If you're a woman of a certain age, chances are your formative years were marked by a barrage of very mixed advertising images about what it meant to lead a proper feminine life. How much power does advertising wield with respect to shaping the culture? Jan Kurtz, Curator of American Advertising Museum in Portland, Oregon reports, "Advertising is a very conscious attempt to depict a fantasy lifestyle, so it exacerbates the cultural trends."[16]

How much power does advertising wield? A lot. How much power does God's Word wield? A lot more! Advertising is out to change the outside of us (buying, eating, dressing, exercising), while the Word of God is out to change the inside of us (thinking—attitudes that produce behavior). God's Word teaches discretion and modesty, of which we don't see many examples in the advertising world today.

Discretion and *modesty* are very big words that set very big examples. Discretion includes being wise in handling practical matters, like practicing self-restraint in speech and behavior. A woman who exercises discretion looks honestly at the circumstances and sees the potential consequences of her words and actions. Modesty is not the example of advertising, but it ought to be the example of Christian women. It includes not attempting to call attention to ourselves, and exercising caution in speech, dress, and behavior.

Where will we get our example of a proper feminine life—from advertising or from God's Word? Our choice determines the kind of example we will be to our children.

Father,
Thank You for wonderful words in the Bible like discretion *and* modesty. *May we choose to exercise them in our lives so we will be good examples to our daughters and sons. Amen.*

FOUR

Example

Remember your leaders, who spoke the word of God to you. Consider the outcome of their way of life and imitate their faith.

HEBREWS 13:7

I love the triplet pattern found in this verse, instructing me to do three things: "remember," "consider," and "imitate."

"Remember your leaders"—the ones who spoke God's Word to you. I am thankful for childhood memories of Pastor and Mrs. Rushing, Mrs. Brown, Mrs. Heggeland, my parents, Mary Waldo, Jacky Riley, the Bevers, Roger and Jan Creamer, the Thompsons, the Anchas, and more. From my adult years I think of Beth Raney, Jack and Theo Robinson, Pastor Kent Hughes, and others from whom I have heard God's Word. None of these people are or were perfect, but I am grateful they have been faithful in their lives and in their commitment to teach God's Word, whether it was in a children's Sunday school class, a youth group, a Bible study, or a Sunday morning worship service.

"Consider the outcome of their way of life." To the best of my knowledge, the people I remembered above have continued to walk with God. Unfortunately, this is not the case with all leaders who call themselves Christians, and that is devastating to the people who have sat under their teaching. If the outcome of a leader's life is spiritually ugly, disobedient, or rebellious, it's difficult, if not impossible, to follow the third instruction, which is . . .

"Imitate their faith." Imitating involves copying, duplicating, or mirroring. This verse is quite sobering for those of us who are in positions of leadership—whether we're moms, youth leaders, teachers, or Bible study leaders. Is our faith worth imitating? If they're not old enough already, our children will someday be remembering, considering, and imitating our faith!

Father,
May I be a good example to my children and their friends. May I remember that they will be remembering me, considering me, and imitating me. Amen.

FIVE

Example

*Praise be to the God and Father of our Lord Jesus Christ,
the Father of compassion and the God of all comfort,
who comforts us in all our troubles, so that we can comfort those
in any trouble with the comfort we ourselves have received from God.
For just as the sufferings of Christ flow over into our lives,
so also through Christ our comfort overflows.*

2 Corinthians 1:3-5

When my friend Marti was dying of cancer and she had only a month to live, she gave me the book *A Shepherd Looks at Psalm 23* by Phillip Keller. When I read the book, I realized why Marti had been so encouraged by it. The author's wife had been sick with cancer for two years before she died, and he wrote not as an example of a life untouched by difficulty, but rather as an example of one who had walked through pain and loss himself.

He said that during his wife's illness and even after her death, he was amazed at the strength and solace that God's Spirit graciously brought to his life. In the process of going through his own dark valley with God's help, he was being prepared to minister to others.

Only those who have been through such dark valleys can console, comfort or encourage others in similar situations. Often we pray or sing the hymn requesting God to make us an inspiration to someone else. We want, instinctively, to be a channel of blessing to other lives. The simple fact is that just as water can only flow in a ditch or channel or valley—so in the Christian's career, the life of God can only flow in blessing through the valleys that have been carved and cut into our own lives by excruciating experiences.[17]

Do we want the valleys? No! But when we experience God's faithfulness and comfort even in the valleys, we can be living examples of that to others.

God even in the valleys,
Thank You that as we experience troubles, You are faithful to give us Your comfort and compassion. Thank You that when we have received it and experienced it ourselves, we can comfort others with the comfort we received from You. Amen.

EXTRA READINGS FOR DAYS 6 AND 7
Hebrews 13:7-21; Proverbs 11

7

Obedience

We know that we have come to know him if we obey his commands. The man who says, "I know him," but does not do what he commands is a liar, and the truth is not in him. . . . This is how we know we are in him: Whoever claims to live in him must walk *as Jesus did.*

1 JOHN 2:3-6, EMPHASIS ADDED

Knowing God results in obeying God. But knowing God is much more than mental knowledge.

We teach our children not to play in the street, because we don't want to see them hit by a car. So we say, *many* times, "Don't play in the street." "Look both ways twice before you cross the street." We know that they hear us, because they even teach their dolls or their animals when they're pretending. But do they really *know*? If they obey us, then we know that they *know*! It's that way with knowledge as a Christian. We can read the Bible, memorize the Bible, and even teach the Bible, but if we don't *do* the Bible, our knowledge is only "puff." [First Corinthians 8:1 says, "Knowledge puffs up, but love builds up."] Acting in love and obedience comes as a result of knowing not the words, but the God behind the words.

The low view of God entertained almost universally

among Christians is the cause of a hundred lesser evils everywhere among us. A rediscovery of the majesty of God will go a long way toward curing them. It is impossible to keep our moral practices sound and our inward attitudes right while our idea of God is erroneous or inadequate. If we would bring back spiritual power to our lives, we must begin to think of God more nearly as He is.[18]

As we get to know the God of the Bible, we will act like Jesus, who was an example of humility and self-sacrifice. Living and acting rightly is the best evidence that we know God.

Father,
May we show evidence that we know You by the way we obey You. Amen.

TWO

Obedience

*Then Joshua fell facedown to the ground in reverence, and asked him,
"What message does my Lord have for his servant?"*
JOSHUA 5:14

Are you up against a situation in your life that feels
hopeless? Are you discouraged and tempted to give up?
Before Israel's conquest of Jericho, a closed city, Joshua
and the Israelites must have felt the same way. But they
made several good choices.

The first thing Joshua did was to humble himself before
God. Too many times my first step is to draw up my own
plan—a foolish attempt that occasionally *appears* to help;
but in the long run it is more like putting a bandage over a
wound that needs more serious attention.

Joshua took God seriously. God said that He had
delivered Jericho, along with its king and fighting men,
over to Joshua and the Israelites. Would I have believed
that statement if I were there? Joshua and the Israelites
chose to trust God for the impossible. Although patience
was required, deliverance wasn't about to happen

through sitting back and relaxing—there was some work to be done!

Their reverence for God and their faith in God prompted their ultimate obedience to God. There was amazing attention to detail, including trumpets of rams' horns, marching on the seventh day, and circling seven times around the city—sometimes quietly, but the last time with a shout. There was no room for laziness or cynicism.

When we humble ourselves in prayer, trust God for the impossible, and obey the details, we will see God's victory over the enemy in our lives and the lives of those we love.

Father,
Thank You for the example of Joshua, who humbled himself, trusted You, and obeyed You. Please help us to do the same as we face our own challenges. Amen.

THREE

Obedience

As Jesus was saying these things, a woman in the crowd called out, "Blessed is the mother who gave you birth and nursed you." He replied, "Blessed rather are those who hear the word of God and obey it."
LUKE 11:27-28

When the woman in this story pronounced a blessing on Mary, she was also complimenting Jesus. But by Jesus' response we get the impression that He desires obedience more than compliments. The woman was certainly sincere, but sincerity alone is not enough.

The order of events in this passage of Scripture is no coincidence. Notice the first words of the verse above: "As Jesus was saying these things . . ." What was He saying? "He who is not with me is against me, and he who does not gather with me, scatters" (Luke 11:23). Jesus was cautioning the people against neutrality. He was teaching them that there's a spiritual war going on, and we must choose between two forces. While Jesus is building His kingdom, Satan is trying to destroy it. We must choose between the two, and if we don't make a choice, we are in essence against Christ. As Warren Wiersbe says, "We

take sides with Jesus Christ when we hear His Word and
obey it."

All throughout God's Word we are taught that
obedience comes after hearing. God has revealed His truth
to us, and He asks us to respond to it positively and
actively. Isn't that exactly what we desire from our
children? We want them to listen to us and obey us; the two
go hand in hand. Let's not forget that Jesus began His
response to the woman with the word "Blessed." That word
means *happy*. When we hear God's Word and obey, that's
true happiness.

Father,
May we remember that what You want most from us is our obedience.
Amen.

FOUR

Obedience

To the Jews who had believed him, Jesus said, "If you hold to my teaching, you are really my disciples. Then you will know the truth, and the truth will set you free."

JOHN 8:31-32

Who are Jesus' disciples? Who are people of the truth? They are the people who obey God—the people who hold to His teaching.

The Greek expression for "hold to" (*meinete en*, also translated "abide in" or "remain in") has great spiritual significance in the Gospel of John. We abide in Christ when we place ourselves in him and continue there, drawing life from his words. This produces ongoing discipleship. A true and obedient disciple will find the truth by knowing the one who is the truth, Jesus himself. This knowledge frees people from their bondage to sin.

When Jesus spoke of "knowing the truth," he was speaking of knowing God's revelation to man. This revelation is embodied in Jesus himself, the Word; therefore, to know the truth is to know Jesus. The truth is not political freedom or intellectual knowledge. Knowing the truth means accepting it, obeying it, and regarding it above all earthly opinion. Doing so offers true spiritual freedom from sin and death.

Believers become truly free because they are free to do God's will, and thus fulfill God's ultimate purpose in their lives. As believers, we have the Holy Spirit living within us and guiding us on our journey through life. In fact, in John 16:13, Jesus specifically identified the Holy Spirit as "the Spirit of truth" who will guide you into all truth.[19]

It's so important for us to remember that knowing God doesn't come through intellectual activity—it comes as a result of our obedience to Him.

Father,
We confess that we sometimes substitute knowing things about You for knowing You. Thanks that when we obey Your Word, we really begin to know You. Amen.

FIVE

Obedience

"Now that you know these things, you will be blessed if you do them."
JOHN 13:17

We sometimes hear a mom say, "I feel so blessed!" What might have prompted her to feel that way? A clean bill of health from the doctor? The birth of a long-awaited child? These are wonderful blessings. But we must be careful not to limit our perception of blessings only to what we get. In John 13 Jesus taught his disciples that *obedience brings blessing*. Specifically He taught that blessing comes through humble service to others—hearing God's instructions to serve one another, and then putting the instructions into action.

Two years ago one of my friends died of cancer, leaving three sons who are close friends of my sons. Shortly before she died, I asked if there was anything more I could do. She said, "Just keep in touch with my boys." I took her request seriously, and great blessing has been mine. Whether it's been giving the boys rides, sending cards, praying for them, taking them out for donuts, giving them pizza parties for their birthdays, or gifts on Mother's Day, the joy I have received in doing those things is something I will carry in my heart always.

> We are blessed (happy, joyful, fulfilled), not because of what we know, but because of what we do with what we know. God's grace to us finds its completion in the service we, as recipients of his grace, perform for others. We will find our greatest joy in obeying Christ by serving others.[20]

Father,
Thank You for the amazing blessing that obedience brings to our lives. Our own souls are truly nourished. Amen.

EXTRA READINGS FOR DAYS 6 AND 7
Joshua 5:13-6:27; 1 John 2

8

Fear

ONE

Fear

Cast all your anxiety on him because he cares for you.
1 PETER 5:7

This was one of the first Bible verses some of us memorized as children, but even when we have *memorized* a verse from the Bible, it doesn't mean we have yet learned the lesson and seen it worked out in our lives. God wants us to cast all our anxiety on Him. Other words for anxiety could be fear, apprehension, doubt, fretfulness, panic, nervousness, or uncertainty. We've all been there, haven't we? Perhaps you're there now because your child is very ill, your husband lost his job, or you are caring for an ailing parent.

One of the reasons God permits difficulties in our lives is to present us with opportunities to learn and exercise lessons of faith. In Mark 4, Jesus had been teaching His disciples when they got into a boat together on the Sea of Galilee and promptly encountered a violent storm. Even though (1) Jesus had told them they were going to the other side of the lake, (2) He was with them, and (3) He was calm, they still cried out to Him, "Lord, don't you *care*?" (v. 38). We sometimes do the same thing!

After Jesus calmed the storm, He spoke to His disciples about the unbelief in their hearts. He was more concerned about the problem *within* them than the problems *around* them. This God who is in control wants us to cast (throw, fling, heave, or thrust) our anxieties and fears on Him because He cares for us!

God who is in control of everything,
Thank You that You welcome our worries and fears. Thank You that
You are not indifferent to our cries, but that You care for us. Amen.

TWO

Fear

"Do not let your hearts be troubled and do not be afraid."
JOHN 14:27

These instructions not to be fearful, anxious, or in a panic are often a challenge for me. When difficulties happen in my life or the lives of people I care about, it's very hard for me *not* to react fearfully, and sometimes even to stay there awhile.

I have wondered before, what helps us *not* to act that way? Warren Wiersbe's insights into John 14 help answer my question.

> The world bases its peace on its *resources*, while God's peace depends on *relationships*. To be right with God means to enjoy the peace of God. The world depends on personal ability, but the Christian depends on spiritual adequacy in Christ. In the world, peace is something you hope for or work for; but to the Christian, peace is God's wonderful gift, received by faith. Unsaved people enjoy peace when there is an absence of trouble; Christians enjoy peace *in spite of trials* because of the presence of power, the Holy Spirit.

People in the world walk by sight and depend on the externals, but Christians walk by faith and depend on the eternals. The Spirit of God teaches us the Word and guides us (not drags us!) into the truth. He also reminds us of what He has taught us so that we can depend on God's Word in the difficult times of life. The Spirit uses the Word to give us His peace, His love, and His joy. If that does not calm a troubled heart, nothing will![21]

These are encouraging words. God's Spirit and God's Word offer great help and hope to any Christian dealing with fear!

Father,
Please forgive me for acting fearfully. May I be thankful for Your Spirit, who is my counselor, and Your Word, which is my guide. And may I look to You instead of looking to obstacles or difficulties. Amen.

THREE

Fear

He said: "Listen, King Jehoshaphat and all who live in Judah and Jerusalem! This is what the LORD says to you: 'Do not be afraid or discouraged because of this vast army. For the battle is not yours, but God's.'"

2 CHRONICLES 20:15

Jehoshaphat, King of Judah, was about to face a combined army of the Moabites and the Ammonites, two ancient enemies of Israel. When Jehoshaphat received news from some of his men that enemy troops were advancing toward them, he was alarmed.

When we sense an army of trouble coming upon us—whether it's financial difficulties, health problems, or a marital crisis—what is our reaction? Panic, fear, anger? These are normal human reactions, but we run into trouble if we get stuck there. Any of those reactions, left unchecked, will only add to the confusion and intensity of the problems confronting us.

Let's look carefully at some excellent choices Jehoshaphat made in this situation.

- He resolved to inquire of the Lord.
- He encouraged the people to fast and pray.
- In front of the people, he rehearsed who God is and what He had done in the past and asked for God's help, admitting that the people did not know what to do, but that their eyes were upon God.

Through a prophet, God told the people not to be discouraged or afraid, pointing out to them that the battle was not theirs—it was His.

They then gave thanks and praise to God before they saw with their eyes who was going to win.

The amazing conclusion is that the enemies were thrown into confusion, killing each other, and Jehoshaphat and his people were saved! When faced with trouble or crisis, may we, like Jehoshaphat, remember to pray and praise, waiting to see what God will do.

Father,
Thank You for examples of people who, imperfect like us, made some wise decisions to trust You. Thanks for lessons from the past that remind us that You are faithful. Amen.

*Elijah was afraid and ran for his life. When he came to Beersheba
in Judah, he left his servant there, while he himself went a day's
journey into the desert. He came to a broom tree, sat down under it
and prayed that he might die.*

1 KINGS 19:3-4

Do you know how much fear a man can feel when he's
threatened by a woman? A lot! Elijah, an Old Testament
prophet, was a man of great faith. In 1 Kings 18 we read
that he stood up to wicked King Ahab, asked God to
answer him with fire, and struck down 850 false prophets.
The man of faith experienced some incredible victories!

But in the very next chapter we see Elijah as a man of
fear. Queen Jezebel was not happy when she heard that
850 of her prophets had been killed, and she promised to
take revenge on Elijah. In spite of the great victory he had
just experienced, the prophet fled eighty miles *into even
greater danger!* (He didn't know Ahab's daughter was
reigning in that land along with Jehoram.) Elijah left his
servant there and traveled alone into the wastelands—one
lonely and despondent man. He was so exhausted

physically and emotionally that when he lay down to sleep, he prayed that God would take away his life! Elijah was in trouble here. He had taken his eyes off God and had fixed them on himself.

As God so often does, He graciously protected and ministered to Elijah. God sent an angel to give him food to strengthen him for his journey to Mt. Horeb, where God spoke to Elijah and reminded him of His great power, using wind, an earthquake, and finally a quiet voice. Elijah learned that God can be trusted always—when there are great displays of power and when things are quiet. What are you afraid of? What is overwhelming in your life? God can be trusted *always*. Our job is to keep our eyes on Him!

God of the fire and the still, small voice,
It's reassuring to know that even great prophets of the Bible struggled
with fear and disillusionment. May we turn to You in our times of fear
so You can strengthen and encourage us. Amen.

Fear

Since the children have flesh and blood, he too shared in their humanity so that by his death he might destroy him who holds the power of death—that is, the devil—and free those who all their lives were held in slavery by their fear of death.

HEBREWS 2:14-15

Sometimes we hear people joke that they'd rather die than have a root canal. But the fear of death is a real fear that must be faced by every human being sooner or later. A mom reading this might have received news that one of her family members has only a few months to live. Another mom might have a child asking questions about death, or a mother may have just buried her own mother.

The author of the book of Hebrews wrote to people who were immobilized by their fear of death, and he encouraged them with some truths that encourage our hearts today. First of all, Jesus shared our humanity. We all connect back to Adam. But just as sin was brought into the world by Adam, righteousness came through Jesus Christ, who was born into our world as God's Son. And when we believe in Christ, *He calls us His brothers and sisters!*

Second, when Jesus died (with human flesh just like ours, nailed and bleeding on a cross), He called out to God, in faith, "Father, into your hands I commit my Spirit" (Luke 23:46). The last words He spoke on earth were words of *dependence*, and those must be our thoughts and words also. *Jesus needed to exercise faith in suffering too.*

Finally, Jesus' death on the cross destroyed the power of death, and His resurrection promised our union with Him in eternal life! If we ponder the reality of these truths, our hearts will be encouraged.

Lord Jesus,
Thank You that You didn't leave us on earth as orphans, but You died so we could have life. Even though our physical bodies will someday die, may we be encouraged that You shared our humanity and trusted God, and because of Your resurrection, we will share in Your eternal life! Amen.

EXTRA READINGS FOR DAYS 6 AND 7
Psalm 34; Psalm 46

9

Food

ONE

Food

I tell you the truth, if you have faith as small as a mustard seed, you can say to this mountain, 'Move from here to there' and it will move. Nothing will be impossible for you."
MATTHEW 17:20

My family has this running joke about mustard. I like the plain variety, and everyone else in the family (my husband and three sons) likes the Grey Poupon. So I shop for both kinds, and since I'm the only female in our family, the boys call mine the "sissy mustard"!

Here's a life lesson you can teach your kids the next time they squeeze mustard on a hot dog: even though the mustard seed is extremely small, the mustard plant can reach a height of fifteen feet. It sounds more like a tree, but it's in the plant family. From the seeds of the mustard plant we can make a sauce, mild or spicy, to use in our favorite sandwiches.

When Jesus lived on earth, He taught His disciples spiritual truths by talking about common things they frequently saw or used. Mustard came up several times in his teaching. In Matthew 17 Jesus grieved over the lack of faith He saw in His disciples and told them that if they had faith as small as a mustard seed, they would do great things for God.

Great faith has very small beginnings. It begins with opening ourselves to God. When we come to Him and expose our dark hearts to the light of His grace and truth, the roots of our lives are forced down into the soil of His amazing love. Then, miraculously, just as green shoots of the mustard plant come out of the ground and grow to heights of four to fifteen feet, we see shoots of faith appearing in our lives.

Father,
Thank You for teaching us big lessons through small things. May we place our faith in You and watch for growth in our lives. Amen.

TWO

Food

*You are the salt of the earth. But if the salt loses its saltiness—
how can it be made salty again? It is no longer good
for anything, except to be thrown out and trampled by men."*
MATTHEW 5:13

How do you use salt in your home? Yesterday it was one of the ingredients I added to make Irish Soda Bread, and later in the day I used it when I prepared lasagna. In the winter we sometimes sprinkle salt on our front step and walkway to melt the ice.

Salt was a very important commodity in Old Testament times. Similar to today, it was used to season foods, but it was also used to preserve and purify. The expression *covenant of salt* meant the same thing as an everlasting covenant, representing faithfulness, dependability, and preservation.

When Jesus taught that His believers are the salt of the earth, He was speaking of these same properties of salt—faithfulness, dependability, and preservation. Just as salt gives flavor to our food, we Christians are God's salt in the world today. We are distinctive, and we have a unique flavor. If we lose our saltiness, we will not be helpful in building up God's kingdom.

Salt makes food very appetizing when used in appropriate measures. But if you've ever had the top of the salt shaker fly off when you were sprinkling salt on your scrambled eggs, you know that too much of a good thing can be less than appetizing! Likewise, as believers we realize that just dumping salt is not effective. Since we are supposed to be appetizing, not offensive, we are wise to pray that we will live lives that are gracious and faithful to God's truth.

God,
Thank You that You don't ask us to be salty on our own. May we walk close to You so our lives will be both tasty and tasteful. Amen.

If you find honey, eat just enough—too much of it, and you will vomit.
PROVERBS 25:16

Honey. My mom used to drizzle it over hot biscuits she baked for us on cold winter mornings. I add honey to hot cooked carrots in order to sweeten the taste. Perhaps you use it as a substitute for sugar in some of your own recipes. Simply put, honey sweetens things. But too much of it isn't a good thing. Just ask Winnie the Pooh about that! When moms across the country read Winnie the Pooh stories out loud, recounting Pooh eating a whole pot of honey and promptly getting stuck in a doorway, even children get the idea that although honey is good, too much honey is not!

The Bible uses honey to teach us about perspective and moderation, and not just in regard to food. We need healthy perspective for all of life. The verse directly after the one above speaks to moderation in friendships. "Seldom set foot in your neighbor's house—too much of you, and he will hate you" (Proverbs 25:17). Later in the same chapter, verse 27 warns, "It is not good to eat too much honey, nor is it honorable to seek one's own honor." To be respected or recognized is a good thing, but to go running after it is not.

In Proverbs 24:13-14, a wise father encourages his son to enjoy honey, which is sweet to the taste, but even more, to enjoy wisdom, which is sweet to the soul. Honey brings instant delight, but wisdom brings lasting hope!

Father,
May we be wise and look for healthy perspective and balance in all of life. Amen.

FOUR
Food

*W*hat shall I do?" Elisha asked. "How much food do you have in the house?" "Nothing at all, except a jar of olive oil," she replied.

2 KINGS 4:2, TLB

"Just a little oil," the widow told the prophet Elisha. "That's all that I have in my house." She had lost her husband, and now she feared that her creditor might come and take away her two sons as slaves. Sadly, if the Israelites around this widow had been following the Levitical laws, the woman and her sons would have been provided for. Instead, their situation seemed to be headed in the wrong direction.

When the widow was feeling totally helpless, Elisha asked her two questions. "How can I help you?" and "What do you have in your house?" I appreciate the graciousness of Elisha's inquiries. He wanted to help, and he began with what she had. His questions were not patronizing or pessimistic but compassionate and hopeful.

Elisha then told her to borrow many jars from her neighbors—she had to ask for help. Next she was to pour oil into all the borrowed containers, and then the oil flowed until she and her sons filled the last jar!

Like the widow, we sometimes face situations that we think might have, could have, or should have headed in different directions. When the painful realities of life leave us feeling needy or even hopeless, we can run to God for His gracious compassion and words of hope. He is still the God who sees and provides.

Father,
Thank You that you saw the widow's situation and provided oil for her and her two sons. Thank You that You see me today and that I can run to You and ask You to provide for me. Amen.

FIVE

Food

"I am the bread of life."
JOHN 6:48

It's very significant that Jesus was born in a town whose name means "house of bread"—Bethlehem. All of us eat bread. Whether we bake it or buy it, bread is a staple food—it's basic to life.

Imagine what it would have been like to be on the hillside when Jesus blessed the five loaves of bread and two fish, using them to feed thousands of hungry people. The miracle that happened that day was amazing, but also amazing was the response of the crowd. After seeing Jesus provide them with food, the people wanted to make Him King. Why? Not because they believed in Him, but because they thought He could provide many material things for them. The people were so caught up in having their immediate physical needs met that they failed to see the real significance of the event—that Jesus *is* the bread of life. Jesus knew that they desired the bread more than they desired *Him*.

May we not miss the truth that we need Jesus as our

staple—that the Bread of Life who was born in the town called "house of bread" wants to be our spiritual food each day of our lives.

O little town of Bethlehem, how still we see thee lie!
Above thy deep and dreamless sleep the silent stars go by.
But in thy dark streets shineth the Everlasting Light;
The hopes and fears of all the years are met in Thee tonight.[22]

Father,
Thank You that You are the bread of life and that You can meet all our hopes and fears. Amen.

EXTRA READINGS FOR DAYS 6 AND 7
John 6:25-59; Matthew 17:14-21

10

The Heart

ONE

The Heart

Above all else, guard your heart, for it is the wellspring of life.
PROVERBS 4:23

What is a *wellspring*? It is the source of a stream or a spring, the point where something springs into being—the place where things are created or initiated. What a fitting picture of our hearts, where thoughts, attitudes, and actions are created and initiated. The verse above begins with a weighty warning. More than anything else, we must "guard" our hearts. Not coddle, pamper, or indulge—but *guard*. Whenever I guard anything, I protect it, watch over it, or take necessary precautions to keep it safe.

Our hearts determine our true personality or character. Are we pursuing purity or evil? Are we headed toward maturity or rebellion? The Bible teaches us that the most important thing we can do is to love God with our *whole hearts*—hearts that are undivided and fixed on Jesus. Once we have established that God is the focus of our hearts, then we guard them. Notice the common thread in these verses:

See to it, brothers, that none of you has a sinful, unbelieving heart that turns away from the living God. (Hebrews 3:12)

Come near to God and he will come near to you. Wash your hands, you sinners, and purify your hearts, you double-minded. (James 4:8)

We guard our hearts by running *to* God and running *away* from sin. Then we have a wellspring full of good things!

Finally, brothers, whatever is true, whatever is noble, whatever is right, whatever is pure, whatever is lovely, whatever is admirable — if anything is excellent or praiseworthy — think about such things. (Philippians 4:8)

Father,
May we take the warning of Your Word seriously. You are gracious to fill and cleanse our hearts when we come to You, but we must make choices to run from sin. Thank You for Your Holy Spirit, who helps us. Amen.

TWO

The Heart

I pray that out of his glorious riches he may strengthen you with power through his Spirit in your inner being, so that Christ may dwell in your hearts through faith.

EPHESIANS 3:16-17

What kind of heart do we choose to have? Physically speaking, we can't choose our hearts. We live with the heart we were born with, whether it is strong, weak, defective, or in good working condition. Spiritually speaking, we are all born with sinful hearts (Romans 3:23: "For all have sinned and fall short of the glory of God"). But the good news is, we have a choice about the kind of heart we would like to have.

Left on our own, our hearts are stubborn (Jeremiah 3:17). In fact, the Bible likens us to sheep that have gone astray, thinking they can make it on their own. How foolish! When a sheep refuses to follow the shepherd, setting out on his own, he invites all kinds of trouble upon himself—he doesn't know where the water is, he can't get rid of parasites by himself, and he opens himself up to destruction by his predators.

If we don't want hearts that lead us into evil thoughts, lying, sexual immorality, or theft, we must choose to ask God to cleanse our hearts and fill them with the presence of His Spirit (Romans 5:5). This happens from start to finish by *faith*. By faith we ask God to give us a new heart, and by faith we look to Him each day, exposing hearts that would easily fall into dark things if not regularly brought to the light of God's truth.

Father,
Thank You that we have a choice about the kind of heart we want to have. Thank You that You are willing to change us as we place our faith in You. Help us to guide our children's hearts to You. Amen.

The Heart

Slaves, obey your masters; be eager to give them your very best.
Serve them as you would Christ. Don't work hard only when
your master is watching and then shirk when he isn't looking;
work hard and with gladness all the time, as though working
for Christ, doing the will of God with all your hearts.
EPHESIANS 6:5-8, TLB

"Doing the will of God with all your hearts" (vs. 8) was the key to a slave's ability to keep going in difficult circumstances. Their service was to be motivated not by their own feeble desires to please their masters, but by what was going on *in their hearts.*

For some people, the desire for approval motivates their service. Their efforts only go as far as the amount of positive feedback they receive. For Jesus, service expressed who he was and did not depend on the response of others. Imagine dying for people who might reject your sacrificial act of service. When we serve freely, without expecting the response or approval of others, we are acting like Jesus.

Jesus, the Son of God, knew his origin and his destiny. He knew that he would soon be returning to his

Father. Being assured of his own destiny, he focused his attention on the disciples and showed them what it meant for him to become their servant and for them to serve one another.[23]

In order for our hearts to be in the right place—in order for our headquarters and center of operations to be functioning for God's kingdom, we must do what Jesus did. He focused on His origin and His destiny. When we remember (daily) our sin, the blood that He shed for us, and that He is coming again to take us to our *real* home in heaven with Him, our hearts will want to serve Him regardless of outer circumstances.

Jesus,
Thank You for Your purity of heart. Thank You that although God's plan for You meant death on a cross, Your heart was focused correctly, and You chose to serve your Father. Please give us Your strength so we can serve You from our hearts. Amen.

FOUR

The Heart

Blessed are the pure in heart, for they will see God."
MATTHEW 5:8

God didn't say, "Blessed are the pure." He said, "Blessed are the pure *in heart*." Back in New Testament times, the Pharisees were very conscious of *ceremonial* purity, but not purity of the heart.

The Pharisees practiced ceremonial hand-washings, not for reasons of personal cleanliness, but as extra traditions that they had added to their long list of outward rules. The problem with these washings was that they had begun as a reminder that the people were Jews—God's elect—and thus they were to keep themselves separated from sin. But over the years it had degenerated into a ritual that made them haughty and arrogant.

These washings not only indicated a wrong attitude toward people, but they also conveyed a wrong idea of the nature of sin and personal holiness. Jesus made it clear in the Sermon on the Mount that true holiness is a matter of inward affection and attitude and not just outward actions and associations. The pious Pharisees thought they were holy because they obeyed the Law and avoided external defilement. Jesus taught that a person who obeys the Law externally can still break the law in his heart, and that external "defilement" has little connection with the condition of the inner person.[24]

Ceremonial purity is no substitute for spiritual purity. The washing that God wants to see is the washing of our hearts. First John 1:9 promises, "If we confess our sins, he is faithful and just and will forgive us our sins and *purify* us from all unrighteousness."

Father,
May we focus on purity in our hearts each day, because that's when we see You! Amen.

The Heart

*My heart is steadfast, O God, my heart is steadfast;
I will sing and make music.*

PSALM 57:7

People grow old only by deserting their ideals. Years may wrinkle the skin, but to give up interest wrinkles the soul.

You are as young as your faith, as old as your doubt; as young as your self-confidence, as old as your fear; as young as your hope, as old as your despair.

In the central place of every heart there is a recording chamber. So long as it receives messages of beauty, hope, cheer and courage—so long you are young.

When your heart is covered with the snows of pessimism and the ice of cynicism, then, and only then are you grown old—and then, indeed, as the ballad says, you just fade away.[25]

God is the author of *beauty*. We see it each day, but we don't always notice it. We see it in flowers, snow, colors, the features of our child, or music. We have little chances to create beauty each day.

God is also the author of *hope*. As the classic hymn

reminds me, "My hope is built on nothing less than Jesus' blood and righteousness."

Proverbs 15:13 encourages us, "A happy heart makes the face *cheerful*, but heartache crushes the spirit."

Courage is surrounded like two bookends of waiting on the Lord. Psalm 27:14 teaches, "Wait for the LORD; be strong and take heart and wait for the LORD."

If we want to live a life of dignity and have full hearts for our families, we will frequently run to God, who is the source of beauty, hope, cheer, and courage.

Father,
Thank You that You are the author of all these qualities of the heart.
May You enlarge our hearts for the roles You have given us. Amen.

EXTRA READINGS FOR DAYS 6 AND 7
Psalm 57; Ephesians 3:14-21

11

Listening

ONE

Listening

Listen to advice and accept instruction, and in the end you will be wise.
PROVERBS 19:20

Naaman, a commander of the Syrian army, was cured of leprosy through the prophet Elisha. In spite of the fact that Naaman was a high-level man, he came down with leprosy, a despised disease. The slave girl of Naamans's wife, a young Israelite who had been captured on a raid, had apparently done a lot of listening in her home and "church" while growing up, because she suggested to Naaman's wife that the prophet Elisha might be able to heal Naaman's leprosy. Naaman's wife listened and mentioned the idea to her husband. Naaman listened and spoke to his superior, the King of Aram. The king listened and sent a letter with Naaman to the King of Israel. The King of Israel, however, didn't do such a hot job of listening. He tore his robes and suggested that the whole thing was a silly trick.

But Elisha listened. When he heard that the King of Israel had torn his robes, Elisha sent the king a message suggesting that Naaman come to see him since he was one of Israel's prophets. Then the king listened, and Naaman listened and came to Elisha's house with horses and chariots. When Elisha sent a messenger to Naaman saying, "Wash yourself seven times in the Jordan River," Naaman didn't listen. He went away in an angry rage. But when Naaman's servants reasoned with him and asked him to reconsider, he listened.

All of this listening began with a girl who obviously grew up in a family and community of faith, where she was taught to listen to God. How amazing that it all started with a child's faith!

Father,
May we be listening always to You and Your Word, ready to heed the good advice of godly people around us. Amen.

TWO
Listening

A wise man holds his tongue. Only a fool blurts out everything he knows; that only leads to sorrow and trouble.

PROVERBS 10:14, TLB

Once a young man came to the philosopher Socrates to be instructed in oratory. The moment the young man was introduced he began to talk in an incessant stream. This went on for some time. Socrates finally silenced the man by putting his hand over his mouth. "Young man," he said, "I will have to charge you a double fee."

"A double fee, why is that?" Socrates replied, "Because I will have to teach you two sciences. First, the science of holding your tongue; and then the science of using it correctly."[26]

I used to think that if I wasn't talking, I was listening. But I'm learning that listening is making an *effort* to hear something, and paying close attention in the process. When I dropped off my sixth-grade son for his first day of classes in middle school, I said, "Have a great day! I'll pray, and you listen." Listening is an underrated art. It's not something we do with our ears only; if we're really listening, our minds and hearts are involved as well.

Listening is an extremely important gift that every mom can give to her child. It doesn't cost money, but it does cost time! Ross Campbell, in his book *How to Really Love Your Child*, says:

> Without focused attention, a child experiences increased anxiety because he feels everything else is more important than he.[27]

When we listen to our child, he feels a sense of value and importance. That's a good skill for moms to practice.

Father,
Help us to be quiet long enough for us to truly listen to our children.
Amen.

THREE

Listening

But he listened! He heard my prayer! He paid attention to it!
PSALM 66:19, TLB

I'll never forget God's answer and provision for a prayer I prayed in my freshman year of college. I wanted to attend an Urbana missions conference over winter break, but I didn't want to burden my parents for the money since they were already paying my college bills. So I decided to ask God to provide the money if He wanted me to attend.

Several weeks later my mom called from home saying that I must have forgotten to cash one of my summer paychecks because the company I worked for had inquired about the outstanding check. I explained to my mom where I kept my pay stubs, and when she looked in the shoebox in my closet, sure enough, there was the uncashed check sitting on top of all the pay stubs. Not only did the check pay for the missions conference, but it also covered my transportation back and forth!

Knowing that God heard my prayer and cared enough to provide was a huge encouragement that built up my faith and prompted me to keep praying.

Prayer is an exchange of confidence: we assume the stance of a trusting child and pray with faith that is matched by obedience. God remembers our frailty, loves us as his children, hears and answers our prayers.[28]

God wants our thanks and praise when we experience His listening and His provision. In Psalm 50:14-15, TLB we're taught, "What I want from you is your true thanks; I want your promises fulfilled. *I want you to trust me in your times of trouble, so I can rescue you, and you can give me glory.*"

Father,
Thank You that You, an infinite and holy God, listen to us in spite of the fact that we are deeply flawed and many times ungrateful. May we run to You first in our moments of need. Amen.

FOUR

Listening

"For the eyes of the Lord are on the righteous and his ears are attentive to
their prayer, but the face of the Lord is against those who do evil."
1 PETER 3:12

It's very comforting to know that the God who created the
world and died for me also *listens* to me! When I meet
famous people, I'm not so amazed that they would say
something to me, but I am amazed when they *listen* to me.
God is not like a corporate executive who cloisters himself
in a faraway office, not wishing to be involved in his
employees' lives. The Bible teaches us that He hears us and
listens to us. Astounding! If you are presently wondering if
God is listening, be encouraged by these verses:

*Why am I praying like this? Because I know you will answer me,
O God! Yes, listen as I pray. Show me your strong love in
wonderful ways, O Savior of all those seeking your help against
their foes. Protect me as you would the pupil of your eye; hide me
in the shadow of your wings as you hover over me. (Psalm 17:6-
8, TLB)*

*This poor man cried to the LORD—and the Lord heard him and
saved him out of his troubles. (Psalm 34:6, TLB)*

In my troubles I pled with God to help me and he did! (Psalm 120:1, TLB)

Come and hear, all of you who reverence the Lord, and I will tell you what he did for me: For I cried to him for help, with praises ready on my tongue. He would not have listened if I had not confessed my sins. But he listened! He heard my prayer! He paid attention to it! (Psalm 66:16-19, TLB)

Father,
Thank You so much that You listen and that You never sleep! Amen.

We know that God does not listen to sinners. He listens to the godly man who does his will."

JOHN 9:31

Surely the arm of the LORD is not too short to save, nor his ear too dull to hear. But your iniquities have separated you from God; your sins have hidden his face from you, so that he will not hear. (Isaiah 59:1-2)

God listens to us. He heard the Israelites groaning in bondage, Hannah crying out in barrenness, and David facing Goliath in battle. Psalm 17:1 tells us that God hears the prayers of the righteous.

But there are times when God does not listen, and we are wise to be aware of those conditions. Amazingly, John 9:31 (quoted above) was not spoken by a religious leader, but by the blind man who received sight when Jesus healed him. The blind man had apparently grown up hearing the Scriptures and apparently knew some of the verses from Job, Proverbs, and Isaiah that teach this awesome truth.

Jesus healed the blind man on the Sabbath, and instead of the "religious" Pharisees being pleased for the blind man, they grilled him and his parents with questions, trying to get them to say something that would either get them excommunicated or disqualify Jesus. There was a serious attitude problem here. Look at the contrast between the heart of the Pharisees and the heart of the blind man:

Pharisees (Spiritual Blindness)	*Blind Man (Spiritual Insight)*
Pride	Humility
No Concern for others	Compassion for others
Condemnation	Forgiveness
Hopelessness	Hope
Insensitivity to sin	Desire to repent and change
Anger	Love[29]

The Pharisees thought themselves to be spiritually smart, and yet they failed to realize that God would not listen to them because they were not devoted to Him. We are wise to learn from the blind man that the person God listens to is the person who does His will.

Father,
Please forgive us for the times we've been more concerned with outward show than the inward devotion of our hearts to You. May we come to You with humility, being assured that You will hear us. Amen.

EXTRA READINGS FOR DAYS 6 AND 7
Psalm 66; 2 Kings 5

12

Service

ONE

Service

When he came near the den, he called to Daniel in an anguished voice, "Daniel, servant of the living God, has your God, whom you serve continually, been able to rescue you from the lions?"

DANIEL 6:20

The night that Daniel spent in the lions' den must have been a sleepless one for him. But most likely, he wasn't the only one having trouble sleeping. King Darius didn't sleep either, because he was concerned for Daniel, a man he greatly respected. Darius described Daniel as a man who served God "continually." Let's look closely at Daniel's life to see what gave him the reputation of being God's servant.

Daniel *chose purity*. The Babylonians wanted Daniel to eat the king's diet for three years, which was contrary to the dietary laws of the Jews. The Bible tells us that he "resolved not to defile himself" (1:8).

Daniel *reverenced God*. Even though the king refused to give other wise men extra time to interpret his dream, he gave it to Daniel. What did Daniel do with that time? He and his friends *prayed*.

Daniel *praised God*. After God gave Daniel the meaning

of the king's dream, Daniel didn't rush right over to the king, and he didn't boast. Instead, he praised God for His wisdom and power.

Daniel *testified about God*. When the king asked for Daniel's description and interpretation of the dream, Daniel replied, "No wise man, enchanter, magician or diviner can explain to the king the mystery he has asked about, but there is a God in heaven who reveals mysteries" (2:27-28).

As the king observed Daniel's purity and saw him reverence God, praise God, and testify about God, he was convinced that Daniel was a servant of God. May our lives exhibit the same qualities to those around us!

Father,
As we seek to be Your servants, may we choose purity, reverence You,
praise You, and testify about Your power. Thank You for the example
of Daniel. Amen.

TWO

Service

Now that I, your Lord and Teacher, have washed your feet, you also should wash one another's feet. I have set you an example that you should do as I have done for you. I tell you the truth, no servant is greater than his master, nor is a messenger greater than the one who sent him. Now that you know these things, you will be blessed if you do them."

JOHN 13:14-17

When Jesus washed the disciples' feet, He taught us that service imitates Christ, demonstrates love, is a distinction of being a disciple, and brings joy and fulfillment.

Just before Jesus performed the lowly task of washing the disciples' feet, those same disciples had been arguing about which of them was most important!

Jesus knew that one of his disciples had already decided to betray him. Another would deny him by the next morning. Even this night, they would all desert him. In the next hours they would repeatedly display ignorance, laziness, and lack of trust. It was indeed a sorry lot that gathered in the upper room. Even with good reasons to reject the entire group, Jesus deliberately showed to them the full extent of his love. The actions, words, and feelings that he shared with his disciples conveyed the highest form of love because his disciples did not deserve or immediately appreciate this love.

Jesus knows us as fully as he knew those disciples. He knows intimately of every time and every way that we have denied or deserted him. Yet knowing us, he willingly died for us. Jesus continually displays his love toward us and reaches out to us. He continues to serve us . . . and he guides and encourages us by his Spirit. He serves us as we serve one another. Are we prepared to love one another with the same kind of love Jesus demonstrated for us?[30]

Father,
Forgive us for spending too much time thinking about how important we are, and not enough time serving You. Thank You for the example You left us, and for the love You showed to Your disciples even though they were an imperfect bunch. Amen.

THREE

Service

It was revealed to them that they were not serving themselves but you, when they spoke of the things that have now been told you by those who have preached the gospel to you by the Holy Spirit sent from heaven. Even angels long to look into these things.

1 PETER 1:12

What comes to mind when you think of the word *service*? A friend preparing a delicious meal and serving you at her dining room table? A military person who has contributed to the freedom of our country? A Sunday school teacher who faithfully challenges your child toward faith in God?

I offer thanks to the people around me who work and serve on my behalf, but until reading 1 Peter 1:12, I had never thought to thank God for the benefits I have received through the prophets of old. Old Testament prophets were people of incredible service—not only to the people of their day, but to us as well. They spoke of the salvation that we presently experience, and yet they never lived to see how or when it all took place. Their service must have been prompted by *incredible* faith.

We are privileged to have the benefit of looking back on the first Christmas, Jesus' death and resurrection, and the Word of God that is available to us today. When we see the faith and service of prophets of old, we are inspired to serve God out of gratitude and love.

Father,
Thank You for the service of the prophets and the service of people who passed on the Good News to us. May we not be self-serving people but women who are anxious to serve You, our families, and others around us. Amen.

FOUR

Service

*Because of the service by which you have proved yourselves,
men will praise God for the obedience that accompanies
your confession of the gospel of Christ, and for your generosity
in sharing with them and with everyone else.*

2 CORINTHIANS 9:13

P. Kenneth Gieser, "Ken," was a senior in high school. Ever since flunking fourth grade, he had struggled with his studies. He wanted very much to attend Wheaton College, but his prospects of being accepted weren't hopeful. Since his father had just died, his sister went to bat for him and literally begged Wheaton College to give her brother a chance. The result? He not only graduated from Wheaton College but ended up graduating from medical school, going on to China as a missionary doctor.

To his great disappointment, he became extremely ill in China and had to return home for the sake of his health. His heart sank; he felt as though this was his "second best." But what were some of his accomplishments in this "second best" period of his life? He founded the Christian Medical/Dental Society, founded the world-renowned

Wheaton Eye Clinic, helped begin Medical Assistance Program (MAP), served on the Board of Directors of Christianity Today, the Billy Graham Evangelistic Association, TEAM Missions, and Inter-Varsity, and also founded the Missionary Furlough Homes. He even became Chairman of the Board of Trustees at Wheaton College!

The night he died, he had been visiting at a Christian wilderness camp in New York. His final acts of service were humble—helping the kitchen crew wash dishes and taking out the trash. His son, Dave, reflected, "He went to sleep that night under the stars in the mountains of New York and woke up in heaven!" Ken was a servant who was ready to meet his Savior. What an inspiration for us!

Father,
Thank You for Your servants who are great examples to us. Thank You that You used a boy who once struggled in school to accomplish such wonderful things for Your kingdom! May we serve You with all of our hearts. Amen.

FIVE

Service

He said to them, "Go into all the world and preach the good news to all creation."

MARK 16:15

The life of the one holy Universal Church is determined by the fact that it has the fulfillment of the service as ambassador enjoined upon it. Where the life of the church is exhausted in self-serving, it smacks of death; the decisive thing has been forgotten, that this whole life is lived only in the exercise of what we called the church's service as ambassador. A church that recognizes its commission will neither desire nor be able to petrify in any of its functions, to be the church for its own sake. There is the "Christ-believing group"; but this group is sent out: "Go and preach the gospel!" It does not say, "Go and celebrate services!" "Go and edify yourselves with the sermon!" "Go and celebrate the sacraments!" "Go and present yourselves in a liturgy, which perhaps repeats the heavenly liturgy!" "Go and devise a theology which may gloriously unfold like the Summa of St. Thomas!" Of course, there is nothing to forbid all this for its own sake! In it all, the one thing must prevail: "Proclaim the gospel to every creature!"[31]

These words, taken from Karl Barth's *Dogmatics in Outline*, are very penetrating for the Christian believer and the Christian church. It's important to study the Bible, and we need to gather together for worship and communion. But in all my busyness and plans I must remember that the last words Jesus spoke before ascending to heaven were, "Preach the good news to all creation."

Father,
May my service to You include sharing Your Good News. Amen.

EXTRA READINGS FOR DAYS 6 AND 7
Daniel 6; John 13:1-17

13

Light

ONE

Light

*For you were once darkness, but now you are light in the Lord.
Live as children of light (for the fruit of the light consists in all
goodness, righteousness and truth) and find out what pleases the Lord.
Have nothing to do with the fruitless deeds of darkness, but rather
expose them. For it is shameful even to mention what the disobedient
do in secret. But everything exposed by the light becomes visible, for it
is light that makes everything visible. This is why it is said: "Wake
up, O sleeper, rise from the dead, and Christ will shine on you."*

EPHESIANS 5:8-14

Imagine for a moment the contrast between a sunny day at
the beach with sunlight reflecting off the water, and a day
spent crawling around in dark underground caverns. God's
Word teaches us that a Christian's life ought to be as
different from the world as light is from darkness.

Jesus is the source of our light. As He said in John 8:12,
"I am the light of the world." Throughout the New
Testament, faithful followers of Christ are called "children
of the light." God always deals with us in terms of our
position. He knows that once we walked in darkness, but
now, through our faith in Christ, we have become children

of light. Our position in Christ is the basis for our behavior. Whereas darkness produces sin, the light of Christ produces "goodness, righteousness and truth." Our children know we are not perfect, but when we moms are children of the light, *our* children will see evidence of goodness, righteousness, and truth in us.

I love the words of a contemporary song included in some of our hymnals today:

> *I want to walk as a child of the light;*
> *I want to follow Jesus.*
> *God set the stars to give light to the world;*
> *The star of my life is Jesus.*
> *In Him there is no darkness at all;*
> *The night and the day are both alike.*
> *The Lamb is the light of the city of God:*
> *Shine in my heart, Lord Jesus.*[32]

God of Light,
Please shine in my heart as I follow You. Amen.

TWO

Light

*When Jesus spoke again to the people, he said, "I am the light
of the world. Whoever follows me will never walk in darkness,
but will have the light of life."*

JOHN 8:12

While watching some recent TV coverage of downhill
skiing, I enjoyed seeing the colorful outfits of the skiers
racing down the white hills. During one run the TV screen
went gray, and I could see nothing. Then gradually I could
make out *some* activity, although not very clearly. Ten or
fifteen seconds later, everything was clear and bright again.
The announcer explained what had happened. The skier
began his run in the sun, went through a patch of dense fog,
and then skied into another area of hazy mist before coming
back out into the sun. As you can imagine, I enjoyed the
event best when I could see it clearly.

Our lives are like that. Sin has a way of making things
hazy, cloudy, or dark. We need the light of Jesus to lift the
fog and darkness and help us see our way clearly. We don't
find a clearly lit path by following rules—we find it by
following *Him*. The more time we spend getting to know

God through reading His Word, the more His light will shine in our hearts.

When light can easily pass through a material—a piece of glass, for example—we describe it as *transparent*. Some materials, such as waxed paper, let only some light through. Those are *translucent*. Other materials, such as bricks, do not let any light pass through. These are *opaque*. As Christian moms, we can be transparent if we follow Jesus closely. When we follow His light, it shines through with brightness and color to those around us.

Father,
May I follow You closely so that Your light will fill me and I will reflect You to my children. Amen.

THREE
Light

"Your eye is the lamp of your body. When your eyes are good,
your whole body also is full of light. But when they are bad,
your body also is full of darkness."

LUKE 11:34

Human eyes are the most sophisticated cameras in the whole world. Graciously given to us by our Creator, we did not have to pay for them. Light is traveling all around us, but we wouldn't be able to see it if our eyes couldn't bend the light and form images for us to see.

When a ray of light first meets the eye, it falls on the cornea, which bends the light, so it will go through the pupil and iris to the flexible lens. The lens adjusts so that light patterns focus correctly on the retina. From there the image is carried to the brain by the optic nerves. The brain decodes all these messages and tells us what we are seeing. God has made us amazingly complex!

In the same way that light surrounds our physical bodies, God's light shines all around our souls. But before it can change us, it must enter our lives. In Psalm 119:130

we read, "The entrance of your words gives light; it gives understanding to the simple."

Since our eyes are organs of vision, we must be careful about what we observe, and as moms we also need to protect the eyes of our children. It's our responsibility to seek out the wholesome and to run from the destructive. Of course, our eyes should daily be in God's Word, because only the Word of God, used by the Spirit of God, has the power to bend the light of Jesus into our souls.

Light of the world,
Thank You that Your light is always available and that it gives us
understanding. May our eyes turn away from the unwholesome things
of this world but spend time in Your Word, which changes us when it
enters our lives. Amen.

FOUR

Light

But this precious treasure — this light and power that now shine within us — is held in a perishable container, that is, in our weak bodies. Everyone can see that the glorious power within must be from God and is not our own.

2 CORINTHIANS 4:7, TLB

It's easy to fall into a false belief that in order for us to reflect the light of Jesus, we need to do it from a position of strength. But God says that His strength is made perfect in our weakness (2 Corinthians 12:9). It's probably much more obvious that way.

A story from Susan Hunt's book *A True Woman* illustrates this principle:

> When my friend Sharon Kraemer was diagnosed with cancer, her response was, "I am confident that God will use this to take me deeper into His love for me." I didn't see Sharon until several weeks after surgery and several rounds of chemotherapy, and at my first sight of her I gasped. It was not because her body and her hair were so thin. My shock was because Sharon absolutely glowed with peace and love. She was awash with an undeniable radiance. I could only exclaim, "Sharon, you

must have been spending some incredible time with the Lord." She did not need to reply. The evidence was there. This is the essence of the true woman. Regardless of the time in history when she inhabits this earth, she is one who lives in the presence of glory. Her redeemed character is shaped and driven by God's Word and Spirit. Because she is the very dwelling place of the Lord God, her reflection of Him is manifested in every relationship and circumstance of life. The distinguishing characteristic of her life is His presence in her radiating out to all who see her.[33]

God of light and power,
Thank You that we don't need to feel embarrassed about our lack of strength, health, wealth, or intelligence. Thank You that Your light can shine forth from our weak, perishable bodies. Amen.

FIVE

Light

"Let your light shine before men, that they may see your good deeds and praise your Father in heaven."
MATTHEW 5:16

My pastor, Kent Hughes, had an interesting experience when flying back to Chicago from a missions conference in California. He had been busy the whole week and was looking forward to reading C.S. Lewis's *Letters to Malcolm*, but as he got on the plane he prayed, "Lord, if You want me to share Christ with someone, I'm willing." When he sat down, the seat next to him was already occupied by a young man who was reading an Isaac Asimov novel. Pastor Hughes took out his book and said, "Are you enjoying your book?" The result? He didn't even remember the jet taking off or the in-flight meal as he shared Christ with a young man who lived within five blocks of Pastor Hughes's former residence in California. It was the shortest trip to Chicago he had ever taken. He was so caught up in a divine appointment that he left his copy of *Letters to Malcolm* on the plane!

Being a light for Christ is often not convenient or easy.

John the Baptist was certainly an example of that! John was sent out to be a witness to Jesus Christ, telling people that the Light had come into the world. There were three important things that John the Baptist taught (as quoted or implied in John's Gospel), and they are important for us to understand if we want to be witnesses for Jesus:

1. Jesus is eternal (John 1:15).
2. Jesus is full of grace and truth (John 1:16-17).
3. Jesus is the way to God (John 1:18).

Our focus must always be on *Jesus*.

Father,
May we be good students of Your Word so that we will be ready to share Your light and truth with others who do not know You. Amen.

EXTRA READINGS FOR DAYS 6 AND 7
Psalm 27; Ephesians 5:1-21

165

[1]Dr. Paul Brand and Philip Yancey, *Fearfully and Wonderfully Made* (Grand Rapids, Mich.: Zondervan, 1980). p. 206.

[2]Myers, *Handel's Messiah, A Touchstone of Taste* (New York: Octagon Books, 1971), p. 63.

[3]R. Kent Hughes, *Hebrews*, Volume I (Wheaton, Ill.: Crossway Books, 1993), p. 100.

[4]Phillip W. Keller, *A Shepherd Looks at Psalm 23* (Grand Rapids, Mich.: Zondervan, 1970) p. 60.

[5]Kurt Kaiser, "Where Shall I Run?." Word Music, 1971.

[6]R. Kent Hughes, *1,001 Great Stories & Quotes* (Wheaton, Ill.: Tyndale House, 1998), p. 188.

[7]R. Kent Hughes, *James* (Wheaton, Ill.: Crossway Books, 1991), pp. 193-194.

[8]Leland Ryken, James C. Wilhoit, and Tremper Longman III, *Dictionary of Biblical Imagery* (Downers Grove, Ill.: InterVarsity Press, 1998), p. 572.

[9]James S. Hewett, *Illustrations Unlimited* (Wheaton, Ill.: Tyndale House, 1989), p. 380.

[10]"Lord of Life and King of Glory," *Hyms for the Living Church* (Carol Stream, Ill.: Hope Publishing Company, 1974), p. 528.

[11]James S. Hewett, *Illustrations Unlimited* (Wheaton, Ill.: Tyndale House, 1988), p. 195.

[12]Leland Ryken, James C. Wilhoit, and Tremper Longman III, *Dictionary of Biblical Imagery* (Downers Grove, Ill.: InterVarsity Press, 1998), p. 214.

[13]*Life Application Bible* (Wheaton, Ill.: Tyndale House, 1988), p. 1933.

[14]Philip Yancey and Tim Stafford, *Unhappy Secrets of the Christian Life* (Grand Rapids, Mich./Wheaton, Ill.: Zondervan/Campus Life Books, 1979), p. 75.

[15]Ingrid Trobisch, *The Confident Woman* (New York: HarperCollins Publishers, 1993), p. 63.

[16]Connie Lauerman, "Worth a Thousand Words," *Chicago Tribune*, January 8, 1999, Section 5, p. 1.

[17]Phillip W. Keller, *A Shepherd Looks at Psalm 23* (Grand Rapids, Mich.: Zondervan, 1970), p. 87.

[18]A. W. Tozer, *The Knowledge of the Holy* (New York: Harper & Row, 1961), pp. 6-7.

[19]Bruce B. Barton, et al, *Life Application Bible Commentary, John* (Wheaton, Ill.: Tyndale House, 1993), pp. 180-181.

[20]Ibid., p. 276.

[21]Warren W. Wiersbe, *The Bible Exposition Commentary, Volume 1* (Wheaton, Ill.: Victor Books, 1989), p. 354.

[22]"O Little Town of Bethlehem," *Worship and Service Hymnal* (Chicago: Hope Publishing Company, 1957), p. 29.

[23]Bruce Barton, et.al., *Life Application Bible Commentary, John* (Wheaton, Ill.: Tyndale House, 1993), p. 272.

[24]Warren W. Wiersbe, *Bible Exposition Commentary*, Volume I (Wheaton, Ill.: Victor Books, 1989), p. 21.

[25]James S. Hewett, *Illustrations Unlimited* (Wheaton, Ill.: Tyndale House, 1988), p. 25.

[26]Gary Vanderet, *The Skill of Receiving God's Word*, quoted in Kent Hughes, *1,001 Great Stories & Quotes* (Wheaton, Ill.: Tyndale House, 1998), p. 256.

[27]D. Ross Campbell, M.D., *How to Really Love Your Child* (Wheaton, Ill.: Victor Books, 1977), p. 60.

[28]Leland Ryken, James C. Wilhoit, and Tremper Longman III, *Dictionary of Biblical Imagery* (Downers Grove, Ill.: InterVarsity Press, 1998), p. 659.

[29]Bruce B. Barton, et al, *Life Application Bible Commentary, John* (Wheaton, Ill.: Tyndale House, 1993), p. 201.

[30]Ibid., p. 271.

[31]Karl Barth, *Dogmatics in Outline*, quoted from James Hewett, *Illustrations Unlimited* (Wheaton, Ill.: Tyndale House, 1985), p. 453.

[32]"I Want to Walk as a Child of the Light." *The Worshiping Church* (Carol Stream, Ill.: Hope Publishing Company, 1990), p. 539.

[33]Susan Hunt, *The True Woman* (Wheaton, Ill.: Crossway Books, 1997), p. 34.